Teacher's Guide

Jeanne Perrett

Macmillan Education
4 Crinan Street
London N1 9XW

A division of Springer Nature Limited
Companies and representatives throughout the world
ISBN 978-0-230-45586-3

Text, design and illustration © Springer Nature Limited 2015
Written by Jeanne Perrett
The author has asserted her rights to be identified as the author of this work in accordance
with the Copyright, Designs and Patents Act 1988.

First edition published 2015

Page make-up by Zed
Cover design by ai design
Cover illustration by Liz Adcock

Author's acknowledgements
I would like to thank my Editor and team for all their hard work and inspiration.

These materials may contain links for third party websites. We have no control over, and are
not responsible for, the contents of such third party websites. Please use care when accessing
them.

Printed and bound in the UK By CLOC Ltd

2022 2021   2020 2019
10 9 8 7 6 5 4

Contents

Teacher's Guide

Introduction

Teacher's notes

MACMILLAN

Course overview

Course components

Learning Stars is a high level pre-primary course which delivers an introduction to communicative English along with beginning to read, write and spell in English.

There are three levels – *Little Learning Stars* for ages 2 to 3 and *Learning Stars 1* and *2* for ages 3 to 5. The course has a strong drama and role-play strand with the Act it out sections, allowing the children to practise language in a meaningful way and gain confidence in speaking and communicating in a new language.

Pupil's and Activity Book combined

In *Little Learning Stars*, the following activities are included within the Pupil's Book: drawing, circling, matching and pre-writing.

There are four main characters in the *Learning Stars* series: the children Jack and Lily and their friends Horsey the horse and Bella the butterfly. Jack and Lily are brother and sister and live with their family in a house with a garden. In the garden they have a play tent and this is where many of their games and little adventures happen. Horsey is always friendly and funny and often makes mistakes which make the children laugh. At all times the characters are shown in a safe, caring environment within which they can learn and flourish.

Teacher's Guide

The Teacher's Guide provides everything you need to deliver the course. The Teacher's Guide is made up of a printed Teacher's Guide, complete with facsimiles of the Pupil's Book pages for easy use.

The Teacher's notes are detailed but very user-friendly. They give instructions for setting up activities and delivering new language as well as tip boxes and extra activities for each lesson to take account of different class sizes and fast finishers. There are also suggestions for games, drama and art and craft activities, as well as a page of End-of-term activities at the end of the Teacher's notes.

Teacher's website

This provides additional worksheets and templates for craft activities and also has information for parents (with a multi-language area) plus word lists and scope and sequence documents for each level.

Parents' website

http://www.macmillanyounglearners.com/learningstars/english

This provides information for parents to keep them well informed as to what the children will be learning and how. As well as an introductory letter about the course, there are suggestions for activities which can be done at home and word lists for each level of *Learning Stars*.

Audio CD

Each level has audio CDs containing all the Pupil's Book recordings, songs and chants.

Flashcards

There are printed flashcards for *Little Learning Stars* for all the main vocabulary items introduced in Lesson 1. Flashcards for letters *a–z* and numbers *1–10* can be downloaded from the teacher's website in *Learning Stars* Level 1 at http://www.macmillanyounglearners.com/learningstars/teacher.

Walkthrough of components

Website

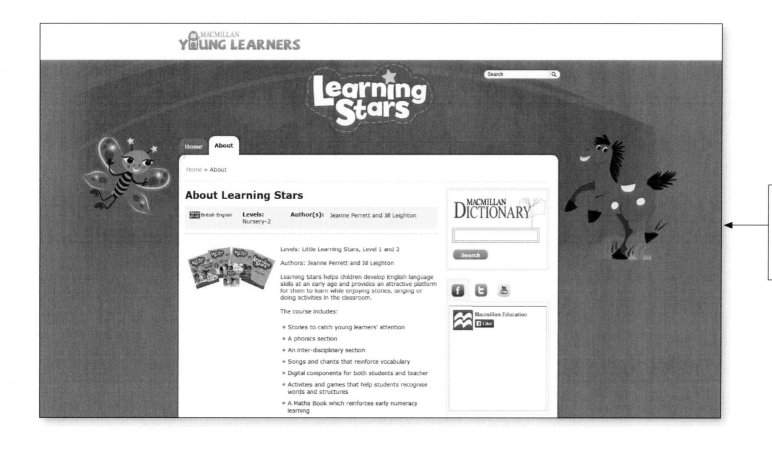

Teacher's website with extra resources, worksheets and templates for craft and games.

Pupil's and Activity Book

Lesson 1

In this lesson, the main vocabulary and theme of the unit is presented. There is a clear audio presentation of the words which the children listen to and repeat. They then sing a song which includes the new vocabulary.

In every lesson there are simple icons for each activity which the children will come to recognise.

In this activity, the children learn the sounds of the alphabet, one by one. There is audio of the sound and an associated word.

The children learn to trace the letter and they colour the picture of the word.

In every lesson the rubrics for you, the teacher, are at the bottom of the page.

The value of the unit is included in the opening spread.

Lesson 2

In this lesson, the children learn a useful classroom routine. There is a song and an on-the-page activity such as matching or circling.

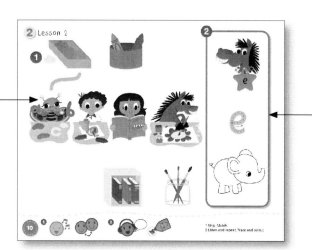

Another sound of the alphabet is presented here. The children listen to the audio and say the sound then trace the letter and colour the picture of the associated word.

Lesson 3

This cognitive activity uses the main vocabulary of the unit and develops the children's thinking skills. There is an on-the-page activity such as matching or circling.

Here the children learn the numbers *1–10*, one by one. Bella the butterfly presents a number. There is audio of the number and the amount is shown in pictures. The children learn to trace the number and colour the pictures. They also sing a numbers song in each unit.

Lesson 4

In this lesson, the children listen to a story about Jack, Lily, Horsey and Bella. The story reinforces the main language learnt in the unit and is included on the CD. After the children have enjoyed the story, they can act it out, using dramatic play to strengthen their language skills.

Lesson 5

In this lesson, a game is presented which relates to the topic of the unit and uses the main language. There is an on-the-page activity (matching, circling, drawing lines or colouring). They can play the same game in class.

Another letter sound is presented here with audio. The children trace the letter and colour the picture.

The children learn to sing the *Learning Stars Alphabet* song. In each unit, they sing the names of the letters they have learnt so far. The song accumulates and by the final unit, they can sing the whole alphabet.

Lesson 6

This lesson is called Big Wide World and here the children are introduced to different aspects of the world around them, such as what materials things are made of, the difference between hot and cold or day and night and things which move.

There is an on-the-page activity and there are suggestions for further exploration of the concepts in the detailed Teacher's notes.

Lesson 7

This is a project lesson with ideas for making and doing something related to the unit topic and language. The craft ideas help to strengthen the children's fine motor skills. There is an on-the-page activity such as drawing or colouring.

Here the children learn a shape and a colour. The shapes can also be found in the main picture of Unit 1, Lessons 1 and 2 and the children can look back in their books to find the correct one. There is audio and a colour song. The children colour the picture.

Review

There is a Review lesson every two units so you can check progress and the children can see how much they have learnt.

The children listen to a recording of some of the vocabulary items from the two units and colour the stars next to the words they hear.

Teacher's Guide

Each unit starts with a clear unit overview, summarising the key objectives of the unit, the target language, the value and the materials needed.

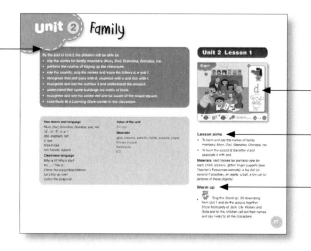

The reduced page of the Pupil's Book provides quick and easy reference.

There is a clear list of aims for each lesson.

Each lesson starts with a warm up activity to help the children 'tune into' English and focus on the lesson activities. Warmers also help to involve all the children at the beginning of the lesson and they can be used to review and scaffold language.

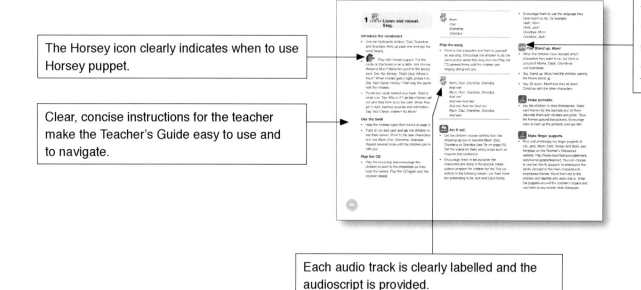

The Horsey icon clearly indicates when to use Horsey puppet.

Clear, concise instructions for the teacher make the Teacher's Guide easy to use and to navigate.

The Teacher's Guide provides the teachers with plenty of engaging activities including games and crafts and simple role-plays via Act it out. There are also one or more teaching Tips for each unit.

Each audio track is clearly labelled and the audioscript is provided.

How to use the course

Little Learning Stars

When we are teaching very young children, our primary concern must be to care for them and keep them safe. Then, within this safe, caring environment we must gradually get to know them, nurture their own talents and skills and then encourage them to develop and learn new ones. Much of our time will be taken up with helping the children to get used to our school routines and to learn to be sociable.

Encouraging children to share toys and school equipment, to take turns, to listen to each other, to be kind to each other; these are all essential elements of our classes. Helping children to become independent, responsible and sociable can, however, also be combined with our other main concern and that is to gently help our little ones to love the English language and to feel comfortable and confident in an English-speaking environment.

All the lessons in *Little Learning Stars* take into account the limited attention span of very young children and their need for movement, games and variety. If possible, speak English to the children throughout the lessons. Although the target language of each lesson may be just a few vocabulary items, try and use English for all your instructions, comments and encouragement. For example, if you want the children to form a circle, say *Make a circle everyone. Hold hands. That's right, very good,* and so on, whilst showing them what you want them to do. When you show them flashcards of the target language say things like *Teddy. It's a teddy. Look at Teddy. Do you like Teddy?* In this way you will create an English-speaking environment where the children will feel comfortable and they will gradually pick up phrases.

Remember to tell the children what they are learning and why. You could show them pictures of children from around the world and tell them that many of them speak English as well as their own languages. This is quite a confusing concept for young children, but they will eventually, over the years, become aware that they are learning something which will help them to communicate with other people, wherever they are.

Using the book

Much of the work you do this year will be through actions, songs and games and there are detailed ideas for a wide variety of classroom activities in this Teacher's Guide. At some point in each lesson, the children will use their books. Apart from the on-page activities (matching, colouring, circling and tracing), these book-based activities help the children get used to using books as learning tools. Show pleasure when you hand the books out, help them find the correct page and let them put the books back neatly in the correct place in the classroom.

Pre-writing

During the year the children will learn how to hold a pencil and trace letters, numbers and lines. They will make letters from plasticine and other materials, they will draw letters in sand or lentils; in other words they will be developing their pre-writing skills. They will not be expected to learn to write whole words. That will come later.

Review

There are regular review pages in *Little Learning Stars*. These are not tests and they are not assessments. They are reviews and their purpose is to make the children feel confident and show them how much they remember. They also serve to help you realise which children need more help with certain language. At no point will the children be tested in this year.

Classroom and daily routines

In each unit of *Little Learning Stars*, the children learn a useful classroom routine or life skill such as pushing their chairs under the tables, washing their hands before they eat and taking their shoes off when indoors at home. They learn songs about these routines and skills and these songs include natural language. As with the letters of the alphabet, it is enough for them to be able to sing these phrases.

Big Wide World

In these lessons, we introduce a variety of topics about the world around us: which things move, which animals are awake at night, what we use bricks for, which things are made of wood, etc. They are designed to increase the children's knowledge of the physical world and can be developed into longer projects.

Craft work and projects

In each unit, there are ideas for craft work related to the unit theme. At this age the actual process of doing craft work is as important as the finished products. Learning how to use crayons, pencils, paints and scissors, and learning how to fold and cut all require certain fine motor skills which the children will develop throughout the year with your help. Decorate the classroom with the children's own work rather than your improved versions. Your work may be more aesthetically pleasing, but it will give the children more pleasure to see their own efforts displayed. When possible, use good quality tools for art work. Even the lowliest scribble looks nicer and feels much better to the child when it is done on good quality paper. You can cut round drawings and mount them on inexpensive coloured sugar paper for display as this makes drawings stand out and makes good displays for classroom walls and corridors to allow parents to see what children have been working on.

Using Horsey puppet

Always let the children know that Horsey is their friend and he is there to help them learn English. You can use Horsey puppet to demonstrate activities, say words and sing songs. You can make Horsey get things wrong and show that this is okay and that if he tries again, eventually he will get it right. Horsey can do funny things, but avoid sudden actions which might startle the children.

Horsey can demonstrate kind and thoughtful behaviour too. Make him a good role model, helping you and the children to find things, put things away and fetch and carry. Make sure he listens to what the children say too and responds in a positive way.

Making and playing with a tent in the classroom

In *Little Learning Stars*, the characters have a home-made tent within which they play. It is a 'microcosm', a little world within a world. In Unit 2, there are ideas for how to make your own tent in the classroom. You might want to use this tent as a place to gather and listen to stories, or it could be somewhere that you act out stories and play at make-believe. Encourage the children to keep the tent looking nice. If they feel responsible for their tent and its tidiness and cleanliness, this will help them to look after their own rooms at home. Accept their ideas for decorating the tent: you could change it every week with flowers, drawings, cushions and different toys.

Using the Unit by unit assessment sheets

You can assess the progress of the children at the end of each unit by using the Unit by unit assessment sheets on pages 102–109. Completing these sheets will help you monitor each child carefully and the information will help you make decisions on what needs to be reviewed from the unit.

In the classroom

Dramatic play

By using simple drama techniques such as mime, improvisation, dancing and movement we can help our children to express themselves, to nurture their imaginations and to feel free to play around with language. Children are naturally drawn to dramatic play – they like to act out being at school or pretending to be Mummy and Daddy. Work with this and act out little scenes, stories and dialogues.

Being an imaginative person is not just about 'being creative' in an artistic sense. As we grow, we need to develop inner resources to help us cope with all the changes, variety, difficulties and joys which life brings. In addition to the practical and physical skills we need, we also require strong mental skills. Nurturing imaginative responses in our children helps them to develop their mental strength.

You, the teacher

You are the most important factor in the children's English classes. You are more important than the books, the songs, the activities, the games or Horsey puppet. If you show the children that you like speaking, singing and listening to English they will share your enthusiasm. Show them that you enjoy writing and reading English so that it becomes something they aspire to.

Some teachers feel a lack of confidence when they speak English and some have had little opportunity to practise spoken English. If you are in this position, try to overcome your own doubts and speak as freely as you can to the children. Listen to the songs and the recordings on the class CD before you go into the lesson so that you become familiar with them and can teach with confidence.

The writer Maya Angelou once said 'I've learned that people will forget what you said, people will forget what you did, but people will never forget how you made them feel.' If you teach in an atmosphere of kindness, encouragement and tolerance and if the children feel your affection and protection during their lessons, they will flourish and learn.

If children have fun in the lessons it will make language more memorable and give them the confidence to begin to use the language to talk to each other.

Hearing, responding and beginning to speak English will provide children with all the preparation they need to take the next step to nursery school.

Tips for a calm and organised nursery class

Good classroom management is an essential part of being an effective teacher. Getting it right will mean you and your classes are happier, safer and stress free. Children are calmer and any behavioural issues are much easier to address in a well organised classroom.

Very young children can be unpredictable and are also not capable of good behaviour all the time. By establishing classroom routines and setting some simple boundaries, children will feel more secure and are much less likely to misbehave. Here are some key tips to help you achieve this:

Have a set routine

Establish a set routine for each part of the schoolday so that children know what to do and what to expect. For example, children should know where to hang bags and coats and what to do after this. They should know where to sit for circle time and what to do after they come in from break time. Follow the same pattern every day and talk to the children about the daily routine – when they can have a snack, when they can go to play so children do not need to ask when these activities will happen.

Setting a routine will take time and patience at the beginning of term, but it will be well worth it. You will have a calmer and less anxious class for the rest of the year. Very young children in a classroom environment for the first time need a routine and daily repetition in order to feel secure. This is part of your role as a nurturer as well as a teacher.

In the same way, the children will also soon learn what the icons in *Little Learning Stars* mean, and will know that it is time for a song, or story or a game. This gives the children some much-needed autonomy so they feel they have a little bit of control over their learning and can see what is coming next.

Preparation

Try to plan ahead and make a list of everything you will need for the teaching week ahead. Keep things you use all the time at hand in the classroom such as Horsey puppet, the flashcards, etc. Other time-saving tips include:

- Organise books according to your seating plan to save time.

- Number tables and books (or give them a colour) so it is easy to organise the books for each table. Children will also learn their table number or colour quickly and this will make organising things such as classroom games much quicker.

- Make a box for crayons and pencils for each table so the children can get into the routine of tidying them away.

- Have a place for everything. Young children love to help tidy up and you could make a simple picture chart of a classroom rota: one day one child collects crayons, another day one or two collect books.

- If possible, give each child a tray or a labelled space to put drawings, books – anything which they will take home with them at the end of the day.

Class rules

Make a simple set of rules and explain them on the first day – essential things such as no running in class, listen to the teacher, share and take turns. Explain what will happen if they break the rules and give warnings before enforcing sanctions. Try to emphasise the positive and praise good behaviour at all times. Make pictures of the rules and remind children of them each day – young children do sometimes forget.

Lots of praise

Make your classroom a positive place with lots of targeted praise. Rather than simply saying *very good*, be specific about what the children have done well: when the children are told why they are being praised they will repeat the same behaviour. This bolsters self-esteem and has a positive impact on behaviour. Children love positive attention and will resort to negative behaviour if they do not get it. Make a star chart for each child – or even a general class one at

the beginning of term while children get used to being in class. Give a small treat or a sticker to the child/children who get most stars.

Simple, direct instructions

Make instructions specific and to the point – *Listen to …, look at ..., stand up, sit down, put your bag away*. Again, use pictures to show what you mean and mime the actions, to reinforce your instructions to suit both visual and kinaesthetic learners.

Busy time

Always prepare extra activities for 'fast finishers' and have something in reserve in case planned activities take less time or you need to adapt your plan as the lesson progresses. 'Fast finisher' activities could include a simple game, using flashcards or colouring in. Letting children play with playdough is a great treat for finishing work and will encourage others to complete their work too.

Variety and pace

Very small children need constant changes in activity and they cannot concentrate on one task for a long time. Ideally, you should plan activities in five to ten-minute slots, and be prepared to juggle them, depending on the mood of the class. Small children are affected by lots of things, such as changes in the weather, whether they have had breakfast, etc. and they can also sense the mood of their teacher and their peers.

Children aged two to three cannot sit still for very long so the teaching notes include ideas for physical activities and games, e.g. there is a yoga pose at the end of each unit (see teacher's website) which the children will enjoy trying to copy.

Young children also need changes in your tone of voice to keep them interested. Avoid shouting as this will merely stress you and the children and increase the noise level in the classroom. Also monitor your 'teacher-talk' – the more you do, the less the children will be able to speak English, so after the initial settling in at the beginning of the year, monitor how much talking you are doing and adjust it if the balance is wrong.

Repetition

Young children learn quickly and can absorb a lot of material, but without constant revision they can forget it fairly quickly too. It is important to review previous material on a regular basis. This is why there is a Review lesson every two units in *Little Learning Stars*. You can also build a quick daily revision activity into each lesson. Children actually love the repetition of a familiar song or chant, in the same way as they will ask for favourite books to be read aloud over and over.

Food as fuel

Between the ages of two and four small children will develop very quickly, growing from a baby/toddler into a young child. They will acquire a whole range of gross and fine motor skills and expand their vocabulary in their first language threefold. At this stage the right nutrition is very important, and it is also important to eat regular meals, as they are very much using food as fuel. Make sure you let them have frequent drinks of water and make time for a snack. All small children are very interested in food too, so build this into lessons and let them try new foods and experiment with different tastes. This can be done in the food unit of *Little Learning Stars*.

Child development between ages two to three

This is a time of enormous change and development as children begin to be more independent and start to display their own preferences. It is important to remember that all children are different and develop at different rates, but as a rule this is a short list of some of the things that children will be able to do by the age of three:

- use up to 300 words, around 100 of them frequently, many of which are nouns
- run without falling over, throw a ball and use age-appropriate outdoor play equipment
- follow two-part instructions (such as *Bring your shoes and coat*.)
- listen with interest and recall the main points of a short story
- be capable of simple, imaginative play – such as the *Little Learning Stars* Act it outs
- be interested and eager to know about the world outside the home (while still being dependent on familiar adults)
- enjoy listening to music and do simple actions to a short simple song.

Pupil's Book Scope and sequence

Unit	Phonics	Vocabulary	Classroom routine	Game	Value	Songs	Numbers	Cross-curricular	Story/drama	Project
1 Hello	a, b, c apple, ball, cat	Jack, Lily, Bella, Horsey Hello Goodbye Yes No	Stand up Sit down	Hello/ Goodbye game	I say hello to my friends.	*Hello!* song *Stand up, Sit down* song *Let's have fun* song *Hello, Goodbye* song The *Alphabet* song	1	Greetings	Hello, Horsey!	Holding crayons and colouring
2 Family	d, e, f doll, elephant, fish	Mum Dad Grandma Grandpa me red	Tidy up	Me! game	I'm tidy.	*Family* song *Tidy up* song *Me and you* song The *Alphabet* song *Red tomato* song	2	Things made from bricks	Let's tidy up!	Make a *Learning Stars* corner in the classroom
Review 1	Mum, Grandpa, Hello, Goodbye									
3 Classroom	g, h, i goat, hat, insect	crayon book pencil table chair yellow	Push your chair in quietly	Shopping game	I'm not too noisy.	*Classroom items* song *Push your chair in* song *Look at me* song The *Alphabet* song *Yellow lemon* song	3	Things made from wood	Horsey in a mess	Make a Bella picture
4 Toys	j, k, l jelly, kite, lemon	kite ball teddy train doll green	Put rubbish in the bin	Guessing game	I put rubbish in the bin.	*Toys* song *Put the rubbish in the bin* song *Skip with me* song The *Alphabet* song *Green leaf* song	4	Things that move	Where's Teddy?	Make a puzzle
Review 2	ball, chair, pencil, crayon, teddy, book									

Unit	Phonics	Vocabulary	Classroom routine	Game	Value	Songs	Numbers	Cross-curricular	Story/drama	Project
5 Animals	m, n, o, p mouse, nest, orange, pizza	cat hen rabbit bird blue	Put your books away	Matching numbers	I'm kind to animals.	*Animals* song *Put your books away* song *Jump, skip* song The *Alphabet* song *Blue sky* song	5 6	Animals that are awake at night	Horsey and the animals	Make animal masks
6 Food	q, r, s, t queen, rabbit, sun, tomato	juice sandwich grapes apple water cake white	Wash and dry your hands	Matching shapes	I wash my hands.	*Food* song *Wash your hands* song *Eight cakes on my plate* song The *Alphabet* song *White cloud* song	7 8	How to make bread	Horsey's lunchbox	Make apple tree print pictures
Review 3		sandwich, rabbit, grapes, water, cat, bird								
7 Clothes	u, v, w umbrella, van, window	shoes socks trousers skirt T-shirt black	Take off/ Put on your shoes	Matching possessions to children	I take my shoes off in the house.	*Clothes* song *Take your shoes off* song *How are you today?* song The *Alphabet* song *Black bat* song	9	Self awareness: happy/sad	Jack's red T-shirt!	Make paper dolls
8 Home	x, y, z fox, yo-yo, zebra	bedroom bathroom kitchen living room		Do a role-play	I like my home.	*Rooms* song The *Numbers* song The *Alphabet* song	10	Hot and cold	Where's Horsey?	Make an alphabet necklace
Review 4		bathroom, shoes, kitchen, trousers, skirt, T-shirt								

Unit 1 Hello

By the end of Unit 1 the children will be able to:

- recognise the names of the characters in the book: *Jack, Lily, Horsey, Bella.*
- say and understand when to use *Hello* and *Goodbye.*
- recognise and use the commands *Stand up* and *Sit down.*
- say the sounds, sing the names and trace the letters *a*, *b* and *c.*
- recognise that *apple* goes with *a*, *ball* with *b* and *cat* with *c.*
- recognise and say the number *1* and understand the amount.
- hold a pencil correctly and colour a picture.

New words and language

Jack, Lily, Horsey, Bella
hello, goodbye
stand up, sit down
/æ/, /b/, /k/, *a, b, c*
apple, ball, cat
1, one

Classroom language

Hello, Horsey!
yes, no
Very good.

Value of the unit

I say hello to my friends.

Materials

stiff card, crayons, stickers, pencils, glue, a hole punch, paints, scissors
Horsey puppet
flashcards
CD

Lesson aims

- To establish the context for the book.
- To introduce the characters and say *Hello.*
- To begin to distinguish letter shapes from other shapes.
- To learn the sound of the letter *a* and associate it with *apple.*

Materials: pictures of favourite cartoon characters from television programmes or books; real apple or plastic toy apple, three small flowerpots or boxes; real apples for a snack; brown card, apple shapes (one for each child)

17

Warm up

- Introduce yourself to the children and tell them your name. Make sure that you know the children's names. If the class is new to you, write their names on cards and place them next to the children. Say *Hello, (Anna)* to each child in turn.

 Make name cards.

- Fold stiff card in half and clearly write the child's name on it. Be careful to make the lettering simple and plain – do not use any extra flourishes in your handwriting. Decorate each card in a different way in order to help the children recognise which one is theirs. You could draw something (e.g. an apple, a cat, a flower) and let them colour it or let them choose a sticker.

- Once the children have personalised their name cards, put two or three on the desk and let them choose their own one. Point to the name and tell them that is what it looks like in English. (See Introduction page 11 about craft work and projects.)

 **Listen. Sing.**

Introduce the activity

 Play *Hello with Horsey.*

- Put Horsey puppet on your hand, smile at him and say *Hello. Hello, Horsey!* (See Introduction page 12 for tips on how to use the puppet in class.) Then make Horsey say *Hello, (your name)* and move him as if he is very happy and excited.

- Now go to each child in turn and introduce them to Horsey. Say *Horsey, this is* (child's name). Make Horsey say *Hello, (child's name)* to each one in turn. He could cuddle them, jump up and down, sit on their shoulders or dance on their desks. Always make Horsey act in a friendly manner and never do anything which surprises the children too much. Gradually, as you go around the class in this way, the children will start to say *Hello* to Horsey. Do not insist on this – let them discover how to say it by themselves and praise them when they do.

Play *Horsey discovers the classroom.*

- Use Horsey puppet to find where things are in the classroom. Let him discover the pot for the pencils and put one in, the shelves for the books (e.g. he could read a book and then put it back in its place).

- Then take a pencil and ask the children where you should put it. Try to do this in English, e.g. say *A pencil. Where do the pencils go?* The children will pick up the meaning by your actions. Do not try to make them translate what you have said. If they do not understand, make Horsey take the pencil and put it in the pot. Praise Horsey. Then repeat the action and the question. The children will gradually get the idea of the activity and you can then show that you are pleased they have understood where things go.

Use the book

- Help the children open their books at page 2.

- Let the children have a few moments to enjoy looking at the picture. If necessary, explain that the characters are in a colourful play tent in the garden. (See Introduction page 11 about using the book.)

> **Tip** This tent will be the setting for many lessons and it contains shapes and colours which will be used throughout the book but not in this lesson. The tent represents the play world of the children. See Unit 2, Lesson 7 for ideas on how to make your own *Learning Stars* tent corner in the classroom.

- In Lessons 1 and 2, the main focus is on the four characters: Lily, Jack, Bella the butterfly and Horsey.

- Point to the characters one by one and say their names: *Lily, Jack, Bella, Horsey.*

- Repeat the names several times until the children are able to join in with you. Now point again and say *Hello, Lily!, Hello, Jack!, Hello, Bella!, Hello, Horsey!*

Play *Who's who?*

- Use flashcards of the four main characters. Show them to the children and say the names clearly as you place them face down on a table. Can the children remember which character is in which position?

18

Play this game with Horsey first. Ask Horsey *Where's Lily?* Make Horsey turn over the wrong card. Say *No, Horsey. That's Jack.* Then ask him again, *Where's Lily?* Make him turn over the correct card. Say *Very good, Horsey!* Make Horsey say *Hello, Lily!* When Horsey turns over the Horsey flashcard, make him say *Me! I'm Horsey!*

- Then continue the game with the children.

Play the CD

- Point to the characters and prompt the children to point too. Encourage the children to join in saying *Hello* to Jack, Horsey, Lily and Bella as you play the recording.

TRACK 01

Narrator: *Hello, Jack!*
Jack: *Hello!*
Narrator: *Hello, Horsey!*
Horsey: *Hello!*
Narrator: *Hello, Lily!*
Lily: *Hello!*
Narrator: *Hello, Bella!*
Bella: *Hello!*

Play the song

- Play the CD. Let the children listen then play the song as many times as necessary until the children start to join in with the *Hello!* song.

 Hold up the flashcards of the characters and Horsey puppet as you sing the song.

TRACK 02

Hello, Horsey!
Hello, hello, hello!
Hello, Jack!
Hello, hello, hello!
Hello, Bella!
Hello, hello, hello!
Hello, Lily!

Hello, Horsey!
Hello, hello, hello!
Hello, Jack!
Hello, hello, hello!
Hello, Bella!
Hello, Lily!

Hello!

 Tip Give the children tambourines or drums to bang as they sing the *Hello!* song.

 Play *Say hello.*

- Prepare pictures of favourite cartoon characters from television programmes or books. Hold them up and encourage the children to say hello to them, e.g. *Hello, Winnie. Hello, Dora.*

- Then put the pictures on a table, say *Hello, Winnie* and let the children hold up the correct picture and say hello to you. Encourage them to speak like their favourite characters too.

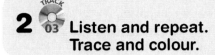

Introduce the letter *a*

- Show the flashcard of the letter *a* and say the sound /æ/. (See Introduction page 4 for details on how to download the letter flashcards from the teacher's website.) Do not say the name of the letter yet. Then write the letter *a* on the board and repeat the sound. Now write the letter *a* several times on the board and, between the letters draw other symbols such as flowers and stars.

 Play with Horsey puppet. Ask Horsey *Where's /æ/, Horsey?* Let him find one and say the sound. Congratulate him. Then ask the children to come and point to the letters and say the sound as they do so.

Play *Where's the apple?*

 Show the flashcard of the apple and say apple. Then play with a real apple or with a plastic toy *apple*. Put it on the table and cover it with a small plastic flowerpot or a box. Put two more flowerpots or boxes on the table. Move them around so they have changed positions. Let the children guess where the apple is. You could play this game with Horsey first, making him get it wrong the first time. When Horsey finds the apple, make him say *Apple!* and dance happily.

Use the book

- Point to Horsey in the panel and draw attention to the necklace he is wearing with the letter *a*.

- Point to the letter in the book and say the sound /æ/. Point to the apple and say *apple*. Repeat /æ/, *apple* until the children start to join in with you.

Play the CD

- Play the recording and encourage the children to repeat.

TRACK 03

a apple
a a a a
apple

- Hand out pencils to all the children. Go around the class helping them to hold their pencils correctly (see teacher's website, http://www.macmillanyounglearners.com/learningstars/teacher).
- Now show the children the letter *a* in their books.
- Show them how to trace in the correct direction, starting at the top of the letter, going round and then up and down.
- Let them colour the apple. Ask them which colour apples they prefer, red or green. Bring in real apples for a snack and let them choose which colour they like best. Show them that we wash apples before eating them.

 Make apple trees.

- Use brown card to make a tree with branches for the classroom wall or bulletin board. Give each child an apple shape and draw the letter *a* for them, within the apple. Use a soft pencil. Let the children colour the apples red or green and help them to trace the letter *a*. Then help them to stick the apples onto the branches of the tree.

Lesson aims

- To review the names of the characters.
- To say hello to each other.
- To start to distinguish letter shapes from other shapes.
- To review the sound of the letter *a*.
- To learn the sound of the letter *b* and associate it with *ball*.

Materials: soft ball, trays, plasticine

Warm up

- Play with Horsey puppet. Say *hello* to him and make him answer. Let the children say *hello* to him and make Horsey say *hello* to them, using their names.

TRACK 02

- Play the *Hello!* song from Lesson 1 again and wave hello to each other as you sing. Continue singing, adding the children's own names instead of the characters.

- Encourage the children to stand up and walk around the classroom saying hello to each other. (See Introduction page 12 about classroom and daily routines.)
- Point to the letter *a* in Lesson 1 and help the children remember the sound /æ/.

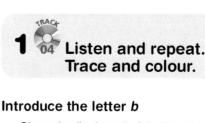

TRACK 04

1 Listen and repeat. Trace and colour.

Introduce the letter *b*

- Show the flashcard of the letter *b* and say the sound. Write the letter on the board and repeat the sound. Now write the letter *a* on the board too. Check that the children remember the sound for *a*.

- Play with Horsey puppet. Say the sounds and let him point to the letters. Make him get it wrong sometimes so that the children start to correct him. Draw other non-letter shapes around the letters *a* and *b* and ask the children to come up to the board and point to the sounds as you say them.

Game Play *Catch and say.*

- Show the flashcard of the ball and say *ball*. Then use a soft ball for this game. Hold it up and say *ball*. Then throw it in the air and say *ball* as you catch it. Now throw it gently to a child. When they catch it, or when they pick it up, encourage them to say *ball*.

Game Play *Letter games.*

- Give the children trays of sand, flour, lentils or salt. Show them how they can write the letters *a* and *b* using their finger.

- Make worksheets for the children. Write the small case letter *a* several times and surround these letters with other shapes, e.g. flowers and stars. Have the children point to the letter shapes. Do the same with worksheets for the letter *b*.
- Help the children make letters from plasticine or dough.
- With chalk, draw two large circles in the playground or place two hula hoops on the ground. Draw an apple in one circle and a ball in the other, or place an actual apple and ball in the circles. Let the children play in pairs or small groups. Call out /æ/, /æ/, *apple* and encourage them to jump into the correct circle. Do the same for the /b/ sound.

Use the book
- Help the children open their books at page 3.
- Point to the panel and the letter *b* on Horsey's necklace and say the sound /b/. Point to the ball. Say /b/, *ball* as many times as necessary until the children join in with you.

Play the CD
- Play the recording and encourage the children to repeat.

> *b ball*
> *b b b b*
> *ball*

- Now help the children to trace the letter *b* in their books. Let them colour the ball. Ask them if they have got a favourite ball and if yes, what colour it is.

> **Tip** Play around with language and use words which are not 'target language'. Take a ball and bounce it and say *buh buh buh buh bouncy ball*. If you have an outside space let the children bounce balls outside and say the letter *b* sound as they play.

Unit 1 Lesson 3

Lesson aims
- To become familiar with the classroom routine of standing up and sitting down.
- To learn the number *1* and become aware of the amount.

Materials: a rug, music; plates of raisins, worksheets for number *1* (one for each child)

Warm up

- Say hello to the children using Horsey puppet. Sing the *Hello!* song again.

1 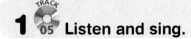 Listen and sing.

Introduce the routine
- Sit on a chair at the front of the class. Stand up and say *Stand up!* Then sit down and say *Sit down!* Do this slowly, several times. Encourage the children to join in with you. Gradually speed up, saying it faster until you are all standing up and sitting down almost immediately.

Use the book
- Help the children open their books at page 4.
- Point to the boy standing up. See if the children can say *Stand up!* with you. Now point to the boy sitting down and see if they can say *Sit down!* Do the same with the pictures of the girls.

Play the song
- Stand up and sit down as you listen the first time and let the children join in with the actions.
- Then play the CD several times until the children are all singing along with you and doing the actions.

Stand up, stand up.
Sit down, sit down.
Stand up, stand up.
Sit down, sit down.

Stand up, stand up.
Sit down, sit down.
Hooray! Hooray!

Game Play Sit down!

- Place a rug on the floor. Let the children walk around the classroom. When you call out *Sit down!* they sit on the rug. You could also play music, pause the CD and then call out the instruction.

2 06 & 07 **Listen and repeat. Trace and colour. Sing.**

Introduce the number 1

- Show the flashcard of the number *1* and say *one* clearly. (See Introduction page 4 for details on how to download the number flashcards from the teacher's website.) Write the number *1* on the board several times, saying the word each time. Hold up one finger and get the children to do the same.

Game Play Number games.

- Give the children plates of raisins. Show them how to take just one and eat it. Of course they will probably want to eat more than one, but you can do this several times. Each time encourage them to just pick one from the plate.

- Make worksheets with the number *1* written several times. Draw other shapes around the numbers and ask the children to point to and identify the numbers. They can point to them or mark them with crayons.

Use the book

- Point to the picture of Bella with the number *1*. Hold up one finger and say *one*. Encourage the children to do the same.

- Show the flashcard of the flower and say *flower*. Point to the flower and say *One. One flower*.

Play the CD

- Play the recording and encourage the children to repeat.

One [pause] *one* [pause] *one* [pause]

- Help the children to trace the number *1* and let them colour the flower.

Play the song

- Play the CD and encourage the children to join in singing the song.

One, one, one.
Let's have fun!

> **Tip** Stand up and dance when you sing with the children. Hold up one finger as you sing, or hold up cards with the number *1* printed on them.

Unit 1 Lesson 4

Lesson aim

- To listen to a story about the main characters which reviews the language learnt so far and introduces the word *Goodbye*.

Materials: clothes for Act it out or photocopied flashcards of the characters, ribbon; Horsey mask template (one for each child) (see teacher's website), straws/craft sticks

Warm up

- 05 Sing the *Stand up, Sit down* song again and do the actions.

- Play with Horsey puppet and make him stand up and sit down. Let the children call out commands to Horsey.

- Tell Horsey he must be quiet now as he is going to listen to a story. Make him sit down quietly and praise him for it. Say *Good, Horsey!*

1 TRACK 08 Listen. Act it out.

- Help the children open their books at page 5.
- Let the children have a few moments to look at the pictures. Help them point to the characters and say their names.
- Show the flashcards for *hello* and *goodbye* and say the words.
- Play the CD and let the children listen and enjoy the story.

 TRACK 08

Horsey: *Hello, Jack. Hello, Lily.*
Jack and Lily: *Hello, Horsey!*

Jack: *Sit down, Horsey.*
Lily: *Stand up, Horsey.*

Horsey: *Yes!*
Mum: *Jack! Lily!*

Jack and Lily: *Goodbye, Horsey!*
Horsey: *Goodbye!*

- Now play the CD again and pause after each frame. Point to the characters and help the children to remember what each one said.
- Then play the whole story again a few times. If they want to, the children can join in with the dialogue.

Act out. Act it out.

- Use Horsey puppet and take the part of Horsey yourself. Make the puppet say *Hello* to the children and call them by their own names. Act out the whole story in this way.

- Now encourage the children in dramatic play by acting out the story and giving different children the roles of Jack, Lily, Horsey and Mum. You could give the children other clothes to wear to make the drama more fun or you could photocopy flashcards of the characters, punch holes in them and tie ribbons so that the children wear the cards like large pendants. (See Introduction page 12 about dramatic play.)

> **Tip** Have a dressing-up box in the classroom. Fill it with old clothes, fancy dress costumes, hats, wigs and pieces of coloured cloth. When the children act out the stories let them choose the clothes they would like to wear.

Craft Make Horsey puppets.

- Make Horsey puppets for each child (see template on the teacher's website, http://www.macmillanyounglearners.com/learningstars/teacher). Glue a mask for each child onto stiff card. Let the children paint or colour the pictures and then attach them to straws/craft sticks.

Game Play *Sit down, Horsey!*

- Play with Horsey puppet. Have the children call out *Sit down, Horsey.* Make Horsey sit on their laps.

- Alternatively, say *Sit down, Horsey!* and the children put the puppets they have made above onto their own laps. Then say *Stand up, Horsey!* and they hold up their puppets.

Unit 1 Lesson 5

Lesson aims

- To play a *Hello/Goodbye* game with a song.
- To learn the sound of the letter *c* and associate it with *cat*.
- To sing the names of the letters *a*, *b* and *c* in the first part of the *Alphabet* song.

Materials: a cloth to cover Horsey puppet, a school backpack for Horsey (optional); photocopies of letter flashcards or letters on small cards (one for each child); cut-outs of cat shapes (one for each child), coloured tissue paper; a cardboard tube or box with eyes, nose and an opening for the mouth, wool for hair and ears (optional) (see teacher's website)

Warm up

- TRACK 08 Play the story from Lesson 4 again and let the children follow it in their books. Then point to the pictures in order. See if the children can remember what the characters say.

1 TRACK 09 Sing and play.

Introduce the activity

 Play with Horsey puppet. Put Horsey under a table or a cloth. Make him appear and say *Hello!* Encourage the children to say hello to Horsey. Then make him go under the table or the cloth and say *Goodbye!* The children say goodbye to Horsey.

- Now make Horsey come in the classroom door and say *Hello*. Make him say *Hello* to individual children. Then make him go out of the classroom and say *Goodbye*. Have the children wave goodbye to Horsey. You could make Horsey wear a school backpack when he comes in, take it off in the class then put it on again when he goes out.

Use the book

- Help the children open their books at page 6.
- Point to the picture of the children entering the classroom. Prompt the children to say *Hello!* Point to the children leaving the classroom and encourage the children to say *Goodbye!*

Play the song

- Play the CD through once while the children just listen.

 TRACK 09

Hello, hello, hello, hello!
Hello, hello!
Goodbye, goodbye, goodbye, goodbye!
Goodbye, goodbye!

- When the children have heard the song once, let them put their backpacks on and line up with you, outside the classroom door. Now play the song again and all march into the classroom, singing *Hello!* Everyone now sits down. Then all stand up and march out of the classroom, singing *Goodbye!*
- Play this *Hello/Goodbye* game several times. You can use this as a chorus every time the children enter or leave the class.

2 TRACKS 10 & 11 Listen and repeat. Trace and colour. Sing.

Introduce the letter *c*

- Show the flashcard of the letter *c* and say the sound. Write *c* on the board several times, saying the sound each time. Now write the letters *a* and *b*.

 Play with Horsey puppet. Say one of the sounds and let him find the correct letter. Make him get it wrong sometimes. Laugh and say *No, Horsey!* until he gets it right. Say *Clever Horsey!* Then let the children point to the correct letters.

- Take the three letter flashcards for *a*, *b* and *c* and put them in different places in the room. Call out a sound and make Horsey gallop in that direction. Then let the children skip to the right place. You could photocopy enough letters or write letters on small cards so that they can all pick one up when they have found it.
- See page 20 and 21 for more letter games.

Craft Make cats.

 Show the flashcard of the cat and say *cat*. Make cut-outs of cat shapes, one for each child. Hold one up and say *cat*. Make the cat say *miaow*. Introduce Horsey to the cat. Make Horsey say *Hello, cat*. Then make the cat say *Hello, Horsey. Miaow.*

- Hand out the cat shapes to the children and encourage them to say *miaow*. Make Horsey say *hello* to each cat.
- Give the children different coloured tissue paper to screw up and glue onto their cat shapes. Ask them in L1 what colour cats usually are, e.g. *Do we see blue cats? Or should they be brown, black, orange, white or grey?* Let them choose which colour they would like their cats to be.

Use the book

- Now point to Horsey in the book and his necklace with the letter *c*. Say the sound of the letter *c*. Point to the cat and say /k/, *cat* as many times as necessary until the children join in with you.

Play the CD

- Play the recording and encourage the children to repeat.

 TRACK 10

c cat
c c c c
cat

- Help the children to trace the letter *c* in their books and colour the cat.

Play the song

- Now write on the board the three letters the children have learnt so far. Point to each one and encourage the children to say the sounds. Now tell the children that each letter has a sound and a name. Point again and say the letter names *a, b, c*.

- Play the CD several times. Encourage the children to join in with the song when they are ready. Hold up cards with the letters printed on them as you sing.

a b c

[repeat x3]

Game Play *Eat the letter.*

- Make a 'letter eater' (see teacher's website, http://www.macmillanyounglearners.com/learningstars/teacher): paint a cardboard tube or box with eyes and a nose and cut an opening for a mouth – make it look funny and friendly (you could add wool for hair and ears, etc.).

- Give each child a card with one of the letters *a, b* or *c* on it.

- Tell the children that the letter eater is hungry and it eats letters. Make the letter eater call out the name of a letter. The children with that letter come up to the front and post the correct letter into the mouth. Make the letter eater say *Yum, yum, thank you!*

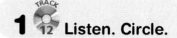

Unit 1 Lesson 6

Big Wide World

1 Lesson 6

1 Listen. Circle. 7

Lesson aim

- To show the language *Hello* and *Goodbye* in a situation which is familiar to the children.

Materials: letter cards from previous lesson; handbags, coats, scarves, etc. for props

Warm up

- **Game** If you have made the letter eater (see Lesson 5), play a game with it and Horsey puppet. Give Horsey cards with the letters *a, b* and *c* written on them. Say one of the sounds and let him post the correct card into the letter eater's mouth. Then let the children call out sounds for Horsey to post.

- Now make Horsey say the letter sounds and the children post the letters. Make the letter eater dance happily when each letter has been posted.

---

1 Listen. Circle.

TRACK 12

Introduce the topic

- TRACK 09 Play the *Hello, Goodbye* song again and march in and out of the classroom. Vary the actions by having the children walk towards you saying *hello* and then turn and walk away saying *goodbye*.

Act out.

- Act out saying *goodbye* to Mum or Dad at the school gate in the morning and *hello* to them again after school. Some of the children could be dressed as Mums and Dads – give them props of handbags, coats, scarves, etc. The others play the part of the children. Pair up the children so that they are in 'parent/child' pairs.

- You could act out a whole schoolday with the children saying goodbye to their parents, entering the school, saying hello to their friends and teachers, sitting down, standing up, then leaving again, saying goodbye to their teachers and hello to their parents again.

Use the book

- Help the children open their books at page 7.

- Ask the children what they think the characters are saying in the photos. In which are the children saying *Hello* and in which are they saying *Goodbye*?

Play the CD

- Play the recording and the children just listen.

1

Mum: *Goodbye!*
Boy: *Goodbye!*
Girl: *Goodbye!*

2

Teacher: *Hello!*
Boy: *Hello!*
Girl: *Hello!*

3

Mum: *Hello!*
Boy: *Hello!*
Girl: *Hello!*

- When the children have listened a few times, ask them to point to the people who are saying *Hello*. Once they understand who is saying *Hello*, help them to draw around the correct circles over the blue dots next to those people (i.e. the children and the adults in the bottom two photos). Use this lesson to reassure the children that at the end of the day they will be saying hello to their mums and dads again.

> **Tip** Children like acting out the same thing again and again. Make time for them to act out the stories and role-plays in subsequent lessons, and to enjoy this natural repetition.

Unit 1 Lesson 7

Lesson aim

- To find and colour the characters Horsey and Bella in a 'hidden items' picture.

Materials: two toys, three cloths; pictures of the four main characters (several pairs of each) (see the teacher's website, http://www.macmillanyounglearners.com/learningstars/teacher)

> **Tip** Laminate the cards, professionally or with sticky-back plastic, so that you can use them again and again.

Warm up

- **Game** Place flashcards of an apple, a ball and a cat around the classroom. Call out the sound /æ/ and let two children run to the apple. Do the same with the other sounds and pictures. Play again, calling out the names of the letters.

1 Find and colour.

Introduce the activity

- Put Horsey puppet on a table with two other toys. Cover each one with a cloth. The children try to uncover Horsey and say *Hello* to him. Make it more challenging by using three flashcards: one with Horsey and two other characters or items from the unit. Slowly swap them around before you cover them so that the children have to follow your action and concentrate.

Game **Play *A memory game*.**

- Print off pairs of flashcards of the four main characters: Jack, Lily, Horsey and Bella. You could mount them on card. Place them all, face down, on a table.

- The children turn over one card and say the character's name. Then they turn over another card and say who it is. If it matches they leave them turned over and the next child has a turn. If it is incorrect, they turn both cards face down. Help them to take turns in this game, turning over just two cards each time.

- Once they have understood how to play the game, let them play in pairs or groups.

Use the book

- Help the children open their books at page 8.

- Say that two of the characters are hiding. Ask them to look, see who they can find in the picture and say the names: *Horsey, Bella*.

- Help them to colour Horsey and Bella, using different colours for each character.

- Finish off the unit by demonstrating the Horse and Butterfly yoga poses (see teacher's website) and encourage the children to join in.

Unit ② Family

By the end of Unit 2 the children will be able to:

- say the words for family members: *Mum, Dad, Grandma, Grandpa, me.*
- perform the routine of tidying up the classroom.
- say the sounds, sing the names and trace the letters *d, e* and *f.*
- recognise that *doll* goes with *d, elephant* with *e* and *fish* with *f.*
- recognise and say the number *2* and understand the amount.
- understand that some buildings are made of brick.
- recognise and say the colour *red* and be aware of the shape *square.*
- contribute to a *Learning Stars* corner in the classroom.

New words and language

Mum, Dad, Grandma, Grandpa, and, me
/d/, /e/, /f/, *d, e, f*
doll, elephant, fish
2, two
brick/bricks
red, tomato, square

Classroom language

Who is it? Who's this?
It's ... / This is ...
Clever Horsey/girl/boy/children.
Let's tidy up now!
Colour the (crayons).

Value of the unit

I'm tidy.

Materials

glue, crayons, pencils, paints, scissors, paper
Horsey puppet
flashcards
CD

Unit 2 Lesson 1

Lesson aims

- To learn and say the names of family members: *Mum, Dad, Grandma, Grandpa, me.*
- To learn the sound of the letter *d* and associate it with *doll.*

Materials: card frames for portraits (one for each child), stickers, glitter; finger puppets (see teacher's website); a doll (or several if possible); an apple, a ball, a toy cat, a doll (or pictures of these objects)

Warm up

- **TRACK 05** Sing the *Stand up, Sit down* song from Unit 1 and do the actions together. Show flashcards of Jack, Lily, Horsey and Bella and let the children call out their names and say *Hello!* to all the characters.

1 13 & 14 **Listen and repeat. Sing.**

Introduce the vocabulary

- Use the flashcards of Mum, Dad, Grandma and Grandpa. Hold up each one and say the word clearly.

- Play with Horsey puppet. Put the cards on the board or on a table. Ask Horsey *Where's Mum?* Make him point to the wrong card. Say *No, Horsey. That's Dad. Where's Mum?* When Horsey gets it right, praise him. Say *Yes! Clever Horsey!* Then play the game with the children.

- Put all four cards behind your back. Start to show one. Say *Who is it?* Let the children call out who they think is on the card. When they get it right, express surprise and admiration. Say *Yes! Clever children! It's Mum!*

Use the book

- Help the children open their books at page 9.

- Point to Lily and Jack and get the children to say their names. Point to the new characters and say *Mum, Dad, Grandma, Grandpa*. Repeat several times until the children join in with you.

Play the CD

- Play the recording and encourage the children to point to the characters as they hear the names. Play the CD again and the children repeat.

Mum
Dad
Grandma
Grandpa

Play the song

- Point to the characters and then to yourself as you sing. Encourage the children to do the same action when they sing *And me!* Play the CD several times until the children are singing along with you.

Mum, Dad, Grandma, Grandpa,
And me!
Mum, Dad, Grandma, Grandpa,
And me!
And me! And me!
And me! And me! And me!
And me! And me!
And me! And me! And me!
And me! And me! And me! And me!
Mum, Dad, Grandma, Grandpa,
And me!

 Act it out.

- Let the children choose clothes from the dressing-up box to become Mum, Dad, Grandma or Grandpa (see Tip on page 23). Set the scene for them using props such as crayons and notebooks.

- Encourage them to act out what the characters are doing in the picture; these actions prepare the children for the 'tidy up' activity in the following lesson. Let them have fun pretending to be Jack and Lily's family.

- Encourage them to use the language they have learnt so far, for example:
Hello, Mum.
Hello, Jack.
Goodbye, Mum.
Goodbye, Jack.

Game **Play *Stand up, Mum!***

- When the children have decided which characters they want to be, put them in groups of Mums, Dads, Grandmas and Grandpas.

- Say *Stand up, Mum!* and the children playing the Mums stand up.

- Say *Sit down, Mum!* and they sit down. Continue with the other characters.

 Make portraits.

- Ask the children to draw themselves. Make card frames for the portraits and let them decorate them with stickers and glitter. Glue the frames around the pictures. Encourage them to hold up the portraits and say *Me!*

Craft **Make finger puppets.**

- Print and photocopy the finger puppets of Lily, Jack, Mum, Dad, Horsey and Bella (see template on the teacher's website, http://www.macmillanyounglearners.com/learningstars/teacher). You can choose to use the 'family puppets' to emphasise the family concept or the main characters to emphasise friends. Hand them out to the children and identify who each one is. Wrap the puppets around the children's fingers and use them to say simple *Hello* dialogues.

2 🎵15 Listen and repeat. Trace and colour.

Introduce the letter *d*

- Show the flashcard of the letter *d* and say the sound clearly. Write *d* on the board several times, saying the sound each time. Now write the letters *a*, *b* and *c* on the board too.

- Play with Horsey puppet. Say one of the sounds of the letters and get Horsey to point to the correct one. Make him get it wrong sometimes. When he does, call out *No, Horsey!* and encourage the children to join in with you. When he gets it right, say *Yes, Horsey! Clever Horsey!* Then ask the children to come up to the board and point to the correct letters. As the children get used to this game, let them call out the sounds for someone else to point to.

- See page 20 for more letter games.

Game Play *Stand up, doll. Sit down, doll.*

- Show the flashcard of the doll and say *doll*. Take a doll into the classroom. Hold it up and say *Doll. This is a doll.* Say *Hello, doll!* Make the doll say hello to you, to Horsey and to the children. Encourage them to say hello to the doll too.

- Now say *Stand up, doll!* Make the doll stand up. Then say *Sit down, doll!* and make the doll sit down.

- Hand the doll to a child and repeat the commands *Stand up* and *Sit down*. The child makes the doll do the commands as you say them. If you have several dolls, let several children play at the same time.

Use the book

- Now show the children the picture of Horsey in the book with the letter *d* on his necklace. Point and say the sound /d/. Repeat until the children join in with you. Point to the doll and say *doll*. Say /d/, /d/, /d/, *doll*.

Play the CD

- Play the recording and encourage the children to repeat.

🎵 TRACK 15

d doll
d d d d
doll

- Help the children to trace the letter *d* in their books and to colour the doll.

Game Play *Find the object.*

- Put an apple, a ball, a toy cat and a doll (or pictures/flashcards of these objects) in different positions in the classroom. Call out the sounds of the letters and get the children to go to the correct object. Divide the class into groups to play this game.

Unit 2 Lesson 2

Lesson aims

- To become familiar with the classroom routine of tidying up and knowing where classroom items are kept.

- To learn the sound of the letter *e* and associate it with *elephant*.

Materials: a box of crayons; long sheets of paper, a glue stick, glitter or small tissue paper balls (optional); a picture of an elephant (optional); small cards with the five letters (*a–e*) (one set for each child), an apple, a ball, a toy cat, a doll, a toy elephant (optional); musical instruments (tambourines, maracas, drums); small boxes, cardboard tubes and a large box to make desk tidies (one for each table) (see teacher's website)

Warm up

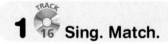
- Put a box of crayons on your desk. Take the crayons out then make Horsey put them back in the box, one by one. Now take them out again and give each child a crayon. Ask them to put them back in the box. Do the same with books from your class bookshelf or box. Then give the children a crayon and a book and ask them to put them back in the correct place.

- Have fun making Horsey put things in the wrong places and call out *No, Horsey!* with the children.

1 Sing. Match.

Introduce the activity

- Give the children long sheets of paper. Draw lines on them in soft pencil. Give each child a crayon or a pencil and help them to follow the line and trace over it.

- You could write lines with a glue stick and give the children glitter or small tissue paper balls to stick to the lines. Display the line pictures on the classroom wall.

Play the song

- Place objects and their containers around the room, e.g. books and a book box, pencils and a pencil pot. As you play the CD, sing and tidy up the objects.

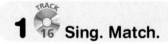
- Make Horsey dance with you as you all sing and encourage the children to tidy up. You could make this song part of your classroom routine, singing and tidying up after each lesson.

Let's tidy up, let's tidy up,
Let's tidy up, let's tidy up,
Let's tidy up now!

Let's tidy up, let's tidy up,
Let's tidy up, let's tidy up,
Let's tidy up now!

Use the book

- Help the children open their books at page 10.

- Encourage them to say who they can see in the pictures: *Bella, Jack, Lily, Horsey.* Say *Hello, Jack! Hello, Lily.*

- Ask if the children can see where the characters should put their plasticine, crayons, books and paintbrushes when they have finished with them. Help them to trace over the sample line from Bella to the plasticine box with a crayon or a pencil; then ask them to draw the other matching lines. Go around the class checking that they are holding their crayons or pencils correctly.

2 Listen and repeat. Trace and colour.

Introduce the letter e

- Show the flashcard of the letter *e* and say the sound. Draw the letter *e* on the board several times and say the sound each time. Show flashcards of the letters *a, b, c* and *d* and prompt the children to say the sounds. If they can remember them, write the letters on the board as they say them. If they cannot, help them to remember by getting

Horsey to call them out. Then call out the sounds again and let Horsey and the children point to them on the board.

- Draw an elephant on the board. As you draw, say *What is it?* Let the children guess. Continue to draw it bit by bit until the whole picture is completed. Then say *Elephant! It's an elephant!* If you cannot draw an elephant put a picture on the board or on a table with a sheet of paper over it. Slowly move the paper bit by bit until the elephant is revealed.

- Show the flashcard of the elephant and say *elephant.*

- See page 20 for more letter games.

Play *a for apple.*

- Make small cards with the five letters *a–e* on them. Give each child a set of the five letters. Now put an apple, a ball, a toy cat, a doll and a toy elephant (or a flashcard of each one) in different parts of the room. Say /æ/, *apple* and let the children go to the correct item and put their card by it. Continue with the other sounds and objects.

Use the book

- Now point to Horsey in the panel and show the children that he has a different letter on his necklace today. Say the sound /e/. Point to the elephant and say *elephant.* Say /e/, /e/, /e/, *elephant.*

Play the CD

- Play the recording and encourage the children to repeat.

e elephant
e e e e
elephant

- Help the children to trace the letter *e* and colour the elephant.

 Play *Musical tidy up.*

- Use musical instruments to make tidying up fun. Give one group of children tambourines, maracas or drums and help them to beat out a rhythm while the others put crayons in pots or books on shelves. Vary the groups so that they all have a chance to be the musicians.

 Make desk tidies.

- Make desk tidies with the children (see teacher's website, http://www. macmillanyounglearners.com/learningstars/ teacher). Help them to decorate small boxes and cardboard tubes with paints and crayons. Then paste these onto the lid of a large box: the boxes could be used for sharpeners/ rubbers, the upright cardboard tubes for putting pencils in. You could make one tidy for each table.

Unit 2 Lesson 3

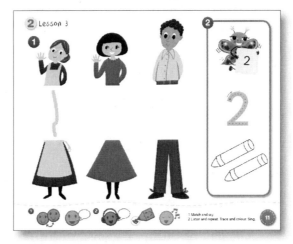

Lesson aims

- To develop cognitive skills by matching the top and bottom halves of Mum, Dad and Grandma characters.
- To learn the number *2* and become aware of the amount.

Materials: a paper bag; pictures of objects the children are familiar with from magazines (or see teacher's website); a plate of raisins

Warm up

- Sing the *Family* song from Lesson 1 again.
- Show flashcards of the characters Mum, Dad, Grandma and Grandpa and let the children call out the words. Put the flashcards in a paper bag and pull them out, slowly revealing the pictures. Say *Who's this?* each time.

- Play this game with Horsey first so that the children get the idea. Horsey could get things wrong so that the children laugh and correct him.

1 Match and say.

Introduce the activity

- Choose a picture of one of the words the children are familiar with, e.g. an elephant, a doll, a ball (see flashcards on the teacher's website, http://www. macmillanyounglearners.com/learningstars/ teacher) or cut a picture from a magazine. You could mount them on card. Cut the picture in half. Let the children put the two halves together to make it whole again. Now add more pictures, each cut in half and put them all on a table. Let the children find the correct pairs to make the complete pictures.

Use the book

- Help the children open their books at page 11.
- Ask them which characters they can see on the left side of the page. Encourage them to point and say *Grandma, Mum, Dad.*
- Have them find and point to the matching bottom halves of the pictures. Help them to trace over the sample line; then ask them to draw the other matching lines between the top and bottom of the people.

2 18 & 19 Listen and repeat. Trace and colour. Sing.

Introduce the number 2

- Show the flashcard of the number 2 and say *two* clearly. Place a plate of raisins on the table and say *one*. Let a child come and take one raisin. Now hold up two fingers and say *two*. Let another child come and take two raisins. Continue with other children and alternate saying *one* or *two* each time. Try to ensure that each child ends up eating three raisins.

- Write the numbers *1* and *2* on the board and say the numbers. Point to *1* and clap once. Point to *2* and clap twice. Now let the children clap as you point. You could also get the children to jump, hop or turn round once or twice.

- Put one crayon on your desk and say *one*. Add another and say *two*. Then count them *one, two*. Do the same with other items.

Game Play *Number games*.

- Play bowling. Place two plastic skittles at one end of the classroom. Give the children soft balls to roll. Encourage them to try to knock down two skittles. Call out *one* or *two* as they knock them down. As the year goes by and you teach more numbers, add more skittles.

- Play hopping and jumping games. Have the children hop on one foot and chant *One, one, one*. Then have them jump on two feet and chant *Two, two, two*.

- Play clapping games. The children stand in pairs, opposite each other. They clap their hands together, first using one hand each and then using both hands. Chant and sing the numbers as you clap.

Use the book

- Show the children that Bella has another number today. Point and say *two* several times. Hold up two fingers as you do so.

- Point to the crayons and count them *one, two*.

Play the CD

- Play the recording and encourage the children to repeat.

 TRACK 18 *Two* [pause] *two* [pause] *two* [pause]

- Help the children to trace the number 2 and colour the two crayons.

Play the song

- Play the CD and encourage the children to join in.

- Let the children get into pairs and dance together as they sing the song again.

 TRACK 19 *One, two, one, two*
Me and you, one, two.

Unit 2 Lesson 4

Lesson aims

- To listen to a story which reviews the language of the unit.

- To act out the story.

Materials: paintbrushes, a cardboard box, paper cups and plates (optional), music, drum or tambourine (optional)

Warm up

- TRACK 16 Tell the children they are going to listen to a story, but first the classroom must be nice and tidy. Sing the *Tidy up* song as you put things in their place.

- Gather the children into a story circle. Take Horsey puppet and make Horsey sit quietly to listen to the story.

1 Listen. Act it out.

TRACK 20

- Help the children open their books at page 12.
- Let the children have a few moments to enjoy the pictures and say who they can see in them: *Lily, Mum, Dad, Jack, Bella, Horsey*. See if they can point to the picture where Lily, Jack and Bella are tidying up. What do they think the characters are saying?

Play the CD

- Play the recording several times while the children just listen.

TRACK 20

Lily: *Mum and Dad!*

Lily: *Let's tidy up!*
Jack: *Yes!*
All, singing: *Let's tidy up, let's tidy up, let's tidy up now!*
[the *Tidy up* song]

Horsey: *Hello!*
Jack, Lily and Bella: *Horsey! No!*

Lily: *Hello, Mum!*
Jack: *Hello, Dad!*
Mum: *Let's tidy up!*
All: *Yes!*
[the *Tidy up* song]

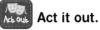 **Act it out.**

- Let the children choose what things they need to be able to act out this little scene, e.g. crayons, books and paintbrushes.

- In the story, Horsey accidentally makes a mess by knocking things over. You could do this safely in the classroom by using a cardboard box as a table and placing paper cups and plates on it. Horsey puppet could knock everything over and then the children could help to put everything back in place. Sing the *Tidy up* song as you do so.

TRACK 16

- Use music to add to the atmosphere of the dramatic play. For example, you could play a fast-tempo song when Jack and Lily are tidying up the tent before Mum and Dad come in. You could bang a drum or rattle a tambourine when Horsey knocks things over.

> **Tip**
> The Act it out activities are not intended to be exercises in rote learning. The children do not need to learn the dialogues by heart. Let them listen to the story several times and they will do their own version. The important thing is that the children are hearing and using English, and having fun communicating.

Unit 2 Lesson 5

Lesson aims

- To develop cognitive skills by matching the letters *d* and *e* to pictures of a doll and an elephant in a simple maze puzzle.
- To learn the sound of the letter *f* and associate it with *fish*.

Materials: an apple, a ball, a toy cat, a doll, a toy elephant; stepping stones made from different coloured paper (e.g. red and blue); plastic letters: *a–f*, a tray (optional), a cloth; cut-outs of fish shapes, metal paper clips, a magnet

Warm up

- Show the children an apple, a ball, a toy cat, a doll and a toy elephant. Prompt them to say the sounds each word starts with. Mime eating an apple. Encourage the children to guess what it is and call out the word *apple*. Mime playing with a ball and stroking a cat and let them say the sounds and the words. Then call out a sound and a word and let the children mime.

1 Match.

Introduce the activity

 Play *The maze game.*

- Make your own mazes in the classroom with stepping stones of different coloured paper (e.g. red and blue). Put a doll at the end of the red pieces of paper and a toy elephant at the end of the blue ones. Give two children flashcards with pictures of those items and let them follow the paths to the correct object.

Use the book

- Help the children open their books at page 13.
- Encourage them to point to the letters *d* and *e* and say the sounds. Prompt them to find and point to the matching pictures. Help them to follow the maze by tracing the paths with their finger and then let them draw lines from *d – doll* and *e – elephant.*

2 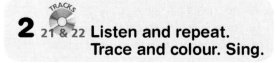 21 & 22 Listen and repeat. Trace and colour. Sing.

Introduce the letter *f*

- Show the flashcard of the letter *f* and say the sound. Then write it on the board several times, saying the sound each time.
- Now start to write one of the other letters the children have learnt. Write it slowly and say *What's this?* Let the children guess as you write and encourage them to call out the sound.

- Play with plastic letters. Put the letters *a–f* on a tray or a table. Point to each one and say the sounds with the children. Now cover the letters with a cloth. Ask the children to cover their eyes and secretly remove one letter. Take away the cloth and see if the children can identify the missing letter and say the sound.
- See page 20 for more letter games.

 Play *The fishing game.*

- Show the flashcard of a fish or draw one on the board and say *Fish. It's a fish.* Cut out fish shapes and within each one write a letter from *a–f* within it. Put metal paper clips on each fish. Now give Horsey a magnet. Call out a sound and let Horsey 'catch' the fish by holding the magnet above the correct letter. The metal paper clip with be attracted to the magnet. Now play this fishing game with the children.

Use the book

- Now look at the book and show the children that Horsey has a different letter on his necklace today. Point and say the sound /f/. Point to the fish and say *fish.* Say /f/, /f/, /f/, *fish* and encourage the children to join in with you.

Play the CD

- Play the recording and encourage the children to repeat.

 TRACK 21

f fish
f f f f
fish

- Help the children to trace the letter *f* and colour the fish.

Play the song

- Review the letter sounds you have taught so far. Remind the children that letters have names as well as sounds. Teach the letter names *d, e* and *f* one by one, associating them with the sound and the picture each time.
- See if the children can remember the first verse of the *Alphabet* song and sing it together: *a, b, c.*
- Play the whole song and encourage the children to join in.
- See page 25 for Teacher's notes on playing the *Eat the letter* game.

TRACK 22

a b c
d e f
[repeat]

Unit 2 Lesson 6

Lesson aim

- To become aware of the world around us and learn which things are made from bricks.

Materials: coloured empty egg shells, cardboard egg cartons with a different coloured card stuck to each one (see teacher's website); a real brick (optional), a toy brick; cardboard boxes or play bricks

Warm up

- **Game** Play a game with coloured empty egg shells (see teacher's website, http://www. macmillanyounglearners.com/learningstars/teacher). Give the children cardboard egg cartons. On each one glue a card with one colour. Now give them some coloured empty egg shells and ask them to put them in the correct carton: the red ones in the 'red' carton, the yellow ones in the 'yellow' carton and so on. This activity helps their fine motor skills as well as developing colour recognition.

1 Find and circle.

Introduce the activity

- If possible, get an actual brick and take it into the classroom. Ask the children if they know what it is used for. Show them a toy brick too and ask them which one is heavier. Ask them which type of brick they think their houses are made of.

- Take the children on a walk around the school and let them find which things are made from bricks. You can explain that we do not always see the bricks in walls because they have been plastered over and then painted. (See Introduction page 11 about the Big Wide World lessons.)

Game Play *Jumping walls.*

- Use boxes or play bricks to make walls in the classroom. Encourage the children to help you build them up. Make the walls quite low and let the children have fun jumping over them.

Craft Make a brick wall.

- Draw a wall of brick shapes. Let the children colour one brick each.

Use the book

- Help the children open their books at page 14.

- Tell the children that the photos at the top of the page show how a house is built. First there is one brick, then builders make the bricks into walls and finally a whole house is built.

- Look at the big picture together. Encourage them to point to the items that are made of bricks (the house, the school and the wall).

- Help them to draw a circle around the items made of bricks.

Unit 2 Lesson 7

Lesson aims

- To make a *Learning Stars* corner in the classroom.

- To learn the colour *red* and become familiar with the shape *square*.

Materials: colourful sheets, tablecloths or large sheets of coloured paper for the *Learning Stars* tent, card stars and other shapes, letters and numbers for the children to colour; sticky tape/glue, a paper tree with large leaves, photo of each child (optional); red items, e.g. a tomato, a strawberry, a red pepper, a red apple, a red rose (optional), circles of card in different colours (red, yellow, green and blue); sheets of paper with the outline of a tomato on (one for each child), red crayons and paints, red paper and glue for each child, a cardboard tube, red cellophane, shapes of red items, e.g. strawberries, cherries, apples, roses, poppies; a square piece of white card, square cards for the children to draw around; a real or plastic tomato, apple and strawberry, a red toy car, a red crayon; red fruit and berries and bowls to make a red fruit salad; red vegetables, bowls and a knife to make red vegetable salads

Warm up

- Look back at page 2 of the Pupil's Book to see the tent which Jack and Lily have in their garden. Ask the children if they would like a tent like that in their classroom. Prompt them for ideas of what they would put in their tent and how they could make one.

- Demonstrate the Chair and Table yoga poses (see teacher's website) and encourage the children to join in.

1 Make and play.

- Help the children open their books at page 15.

- Explain that they are going to make a tent like this in their classroom. (See Introduction page 12 for ideas on decorating and using the *Learning Stars* tent.)

- Use colourful sheets or tablecloths to make a tent in the corner or stick large pieces of coloured paper on the walls. The children can help to decorate the tent by colouring stars and shapes and numbers and letters.

- Put two chairs and a table in the *Learning Stars* corner. This corner could be a place where children take turns to go as a treat.

- Let the children decide what else they would like to put in their own classroom corner to make it pretty. Remind them that they must keep it tidy too!

- Make a paper tree with large leaves and place it on the wall inside the tent. Ask the children to either bring in a photo of themselves or to draw a picture of themselves on a piece of paper. Put the photos/pictures on the leaves around the tree. Say each child's name one by one and the children take turns to go to the tree, find their picture and say *Me!*

Use the book

- Draw attention to the child waving in their books. Help the children to draw their own face on the child, i.e. to draw eyes, a nose, mouth and hair. They can also colour these in.

2 23 & 24 Listen and repeat. Colour. Sing.

Introduce the colour *red*

- Show the flashcard of the colour red and say *red*. Gather together several items which are all red: they could be items in the classroom (e.g. a crayon, a pot, a book) or you could find items which are naturally red (e.g. a tomato, a strawberry, a red pepper, a red apple, a red rose). Point to each one and say *Red. It's red*.

-  Cut circles from different colour cards: red, yellow, green and blue. Place them on a table. Play with Horsey puppet. Ask Horsey *Where's the red circle?* Let Horsey make a mistake and point to the wrong one. Say *No, Horsey*. Praise Horsey when he finds the correct circle and say *Yes, Horsey. Red!* Then let the children play the game.

Craft Make red crafts.

- Make red tomato cards with the children: hand out sheets of paper with the outline of a tomato on them and encourage the children to colour them in red. As they sing the song (see Teacher's Guide page 37), they can hold up their tomato cards.

- Make one-colour pictures. Give the children red crayons and paints, red paper and glue. Let them decide which materials they would like to use and then create a picture with just one colour.

- Cover the top of a cardboard tube with a piece of red cellophane. Let the children look through it to see everything in a red light.

- Give the children shapes of strawberries, cherries, apples, roses and poppies to create their red pictures.

Introduce the shape *square*

- Show the flashcard of the square shape and say *square*. Hold up a square piece of white card and say *Square. It's a square.* Draw a square on the board and say *square*. Give the children square cards to draw around.

Use the book

- Point to the red square. Say *red*. Draw a square with your finger. Say *Square. A red square*.

- Ask the children to open their books at page 3 and see if they can find the same shape on the rug.

- Point to the tomato and say *tomato*.

Play the CD

- Play the recording and encourage the children to repeat.

*Red, red, red
Tomato! Tomato!*

- Show the flashcard of a tomato and say *tomato*. Help the children to colour the tomato in their books red. Ask the children to name other natural things which are red, e.g. apple, strawberry, flower.
- Have the children look and point to things that are squares in the classroom.

Play the song

- Play the CD and encourage the children to join in.

*Red, red, red,
Red, red, red,
Tomato! Tomato!
Red, red, red.*

 **Play *Find red.***

- Place some red items around the classroom, e.g. a real or plastic tomato, apple, strawberry; a red car; a red crayon, etc.
- Play the *Red tomato* song again and let the children skip to the red tomato as they sing the song.

Cookery activities

- Make a red fruit salad with the children. Let them help you wash red fruit and berries and put them in bowls.
- Make red vegetable salads. Chop some tomatoes, red peppers and a little red cabbage and let the children arrange the salad in bowls.

Review 1

Lesson aim

- To review the main vocabulary of Units 1 and 2. (See Introduction page 11 for information about the Review lessons.)

Warm up

 Practise *hello* and *goodbye* with the children. You can start by leaving the room and saying *Goodbye!*; then returning and saying *Hello!* in a very cheerful manner. Then ask a child to go out of the classroom and say *Goodbye!* before leaving the room. Ask the child to come in again and say *Hello!* Repeat this action several times with different children. You can use Horsey to say *Goodbye!* and *Hello!* as well.

 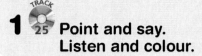
Introduce the activity

- Wave, say *Goodbye!* and go out the door. Come into the room and say *Hello!*
- Sing the *Hello, Goodbye* song.

Use the book

- Help the children open their books at page 16.
- Point to the top left-hand picture. Elicit who the children can see and encourage them to say *Mum*. Ask what they think she is saying. Encourage them to call out *Hello!* Now do the same with the other pictures.
- Tell them you are going to play the CD and they will hear the characters saying *Hello* and *Goodbye*. When they think they know which picture it is, they should point to it.

Play the CD

- Play the first part of the recording. Pause the CD. Help the children find the correct picture (top right-hand picture). Then ask them to colour the star next to that picture. Continue in this way with the three remaining pictures.

Mum: *Goodbye! Goodbye!*
Grandpa: *Hello! Hello!*
Mum: *Hello! Hello!*
Grandpa: *Goodbye! Goodbye!*

Unit 3 Classroom

By the end of Unit 3 the children will be able to:

- say the classroom words: *crayon, book, pencil, table, chair*.
- perform the classroom routine of pushing their chair under the table quietly.
- say the sounds, sing the names and trace the letters *g, h* and *i*.
- recognise that *goat* goes with *g, hat* with *h* and *insect* with *i*.
- recognise and say the number *3* and understand the amount.
- recognise which everyday items are made from wood.
- recognise and say the colour *yellow* and be aware of the shape *triangle*.
- make a finger print picture of Bella.

New words and language

crayon, book, pencil, table, chair
/g/, /h/, /ɪ/, *g, h, i*
goat, hat, insect
3, three
wood
yellow, lemon, triangle

Classroom language

Where's the (table)?
Push your chair in, please!
Look at me!
Colour the (books).

Value of the unit

I'm not too noisy.

Materials

scissors, crayons, pencils, glue, paints, paper
Horsey puppet
flashcards
CD

Lesson aims

- To learn and say the words: *crayon, book, pencil, table, chair*.
- To learn the sound of the letter *g* and associate it with *goat*.

Materials: a large tablecloth; printed or drawn large pictures of a table, chair, pencil, crayon and book on white paper, black card

Warm up

- **TRACK 19** Sing the *Me and you* song from Unit 2. Dance in pairs as you sing.

38

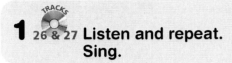 Take Horsey puppet and ask him to sit down quietly at the end of the song and encourage the children to do the same. Demonstrate pulling out your chair and sitting down on it quietly. Encourage the children to copy you. Put your finger to your lips to indicate that they should do this as quietly as possible.

1 26 & 27 Listen and repeat. Sing.

Introduce the vocabulary

- Place a table and chair at the front of the classroom. Put a crayon, book and pencil on the table. Say the words clearly as you do so. Point to them again and repeat the words.

- Now take flashcards of these items. Hold them up one by one and say the words. Give the table flashcard to Horsey and hand the other flashcards to four children. Say *Where's the table, Horsey?* and make Horsey put his flashcard on the table. Look at the card and the table, show the children they are the same and congratulate Horsey for getting it right. Now ask the children to put their flashcards on the correct objects. If they get it wrong, say *No, that's not the chair. That's a pencil.* and let them continue until they get it right. Then redistribute the cards to other children and play the game again.

Game Play *What's missing?*

- Take a large tablecloth and cover the chair, the table and all the items on it. Ask the children to close their eyes. Remove the pencil. Take away the tablecloth and ask the children *What's missing?* They will gradually realise what you are doing. Play this several times, removing a different item each time.

Use the book

- Help the children open their books at page 17.

- Ask them who they can see in the picture (Horsey, Bella, Lily and Jack). Ask what they think Lily is going to do. (She is going to cover the items on the table with a cloth and then take one away.)

- Point to the items. The children may already be able to say the words. If not, say them clearly and encourage them to repeat: *table, chair, crayon, book, pencil.*

Play the CD

- Play the recording. Encourage the children to repeat the words and to point to the items as they hear them.

crayon
book
pencil
table
chair

Play the song

- Now place a crayon, a book, a pencil, a chair spaced out at the front of the class near a table. Point to each one and say its name, adding one word each time, as in the lyrics of the song below.

- Play the CD and encourage the children to join in.

- Play the song again and encourage the children to point to each classroom item as they sing.

- Then let the children dance around the items in the classroom, touching each one as they sing.

Crayon
Crayon, book
Crayon, book, pencil
Crayon, book, pencil, chair
Crayon, book, pencil, chair, table!

2 28 Listen and repeat. Trace and colour.

Introduce the letter *g*

- Show the flashcard of the letter *g* and say the sound /g/. Now write the letter on the board and say the sound as you do so. Take two flashcards, one with the letter *g* and one with another of the letters which the children have learnt so far (*a–f*). Put the *g* card in one place in the room and the other card somewhere else.

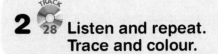

- Play with Horsey puppet. Ask Horsey *Where's* /g/, *Horsey?* and make him gallop to the correct card. Now add another card and hide all three in different places. Now ask a child to find the /g/ card. Continue with the game, adding more cards until you have all seven around the class. Focus only on the /g/ sound at this point.

- Hold up the flashcard of the goat and say *goat*. Make Horsey say *Hello, goat!* and look happy to meet an animal friend. Have the goat make a goat sound *Maaa*. Point out the horns on the goat's head and show the children how to pretend to be a goat, making their fingers look like horns. When the children are miming goats, make Horsey go round and say hello to them.

- See page 20 for more letter games.

Use the book

- Now look at the book and show the children that Horsey has another letter on his necklace today. They will probably be able to say the sound now. Point to it together and say /g/. Point to the goat and say *goat*. Say /g/, /g/, /g/, *goat*.

Play the CD

- Play the recording and encourage the children to join in with the letter sounds and the word.

TRACK 28

> g goat
>
> g g g g
>
> goat

- Help the children to trace the letter *g* and colour the goat.

Make silhouettes.

- Print or draw large pictures of a table, chair, pencil, crayon and book on white paper. Cut them out and let the children colour them in. Then draw around these onto black card and cut these out to make silhouettes.

- Scatter pairs of coloured and black cards around the classroom and ask the children to pick up a matching pair.

> **Tip** Remind the children that they can trace and colour in these school books (i.e. their Pupil's Books), but that we do not always write in our books.

Unit 3 Lesson 2

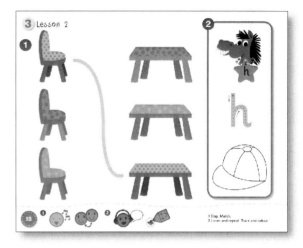

Lesson aims

- To become familiar with the classroom routine of pushing your chair under the table quietly.

- To learn the sound of the letter *h* and associate it with *hat*.

Materials: hats (one for each child), a rug, music; cards with outlines of chairs and tables with simple patterns, e.g. dots, lines and stars for the children to colour

Warm up

- **TRACK 05** Sing the *Stand up, Sit down* song from Unit 1.

- Play with Horsey puppet and make him get things wrong. Ask Horsey to stand up, but make him sit down. Encourage the children to call out *Stand up* to Horsey until he eventually does.

1  Sing. Match.

Introduce the routine

- Place a chair a little in front of a table at the front of the class. Use Horsey puppet and make him push the chair in. Praise him. Then pull the chair away again. This time make Horsey push the chair in noisily. Say *No, Horsey … shhh.* and show him how to do it quietly. Do it a third time and make Horsey do it properly again. Tell Horsey he is a very good horse.

Play the song

- Play the CD and encourage the children to join in.
- Play the song several times and do the actions with the children as they join in with the song. You can use this song as part of your daily classroom routine.

Push your chair in, push your chair in
Push your chair in, please!

Push your chair in, push your chair in
Push your chair in, please!

Use the book

- Help the children open their books at page 18.
- Ask what they can see in the pictures and prompt them to remember the words *chair* and *table*.
- Ask if all the chairs are the same in the picture. What about the tables? Encourage then to find which chairs match which tables. Let them point and show you the pairs.

- Help them to trace over the sample line; then ask them to draw lines between the other two pairs. They can do this with crayons, but if they use a pencil they can easily erase mistakes.

2 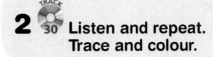 Listen and repeat. Trace and colour.

Introduce the letter *h*

- Show the flashcard of the letter *h* and say the sound. Write the letter *h* on the board several times, saying the sound as you do so. Write several other letters that the children know on the board too (e.g. from *a–g*). Make sure all the letters are low enough on the board for the children to reach them.

- Give Horsey a marker (or chalk if you are using a blackboard) and ask him to find the letter with the sound /h/. Make Horsey draw a circle around the letter. Praise him, saying *Very good, Horsey!* Then give the children markers and ask them to come up to the board one by one to find the letters and draw circles around them.

- Show the flashcard of a hat and say *hat*. Take a hat into the classroom. Hold it up and say *Hat. It's a hat*. Put the hat on Horsey. Say *Horsey and a hat!*

- See page 20 for more letter games.

Game Play *Musical hats.*

- Put enough hats for each child on a rug on the floor. Get the children to make a circle around the hats. Play some music and get the children to dance around in a circle. Pause the music and say *Hats on!* Each child takes a hat and puts it on. Then say *Hats off!* and the children take the hats off again and put them on the rug. Start the music and play the game again.

Use the book

- Now look at the picture of Horsey in the book together. Has he got a new letter today? Point to the letter and say the sound /h/. Point to the hat and say *hat*. Say /h/, /h/, /h/, *hat*.

Play the CD

- Play the recording and encourage the children to repeat.

---

h hat
h h h h
hat

- Help the children to trace the letter *h* and colour the hat.

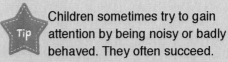 Children sometimes try to gain attention by being noisy or badly behaved. They often succeed. Rather than spending a lot of time on admonishing children, praise good, friendly behaviour, i.e. praise children who listen to each other, children who laugh at other children's jokes, etc.

Make pattern cards.

- Make your own matching games. Give the children cards with outlines of chairs and tables. Draw simple patterns on them, e.g. dots, lines, stars. Let the children colour them. Shuffle all the cards, spread them on a table and let the children match the cards with the same patterns.

Head lice can sometimes be a problem with small children. They are extremely contagious. If a child in the class has head lice, do not play the *Musical hats* game.

Unit 3 Lesson 3

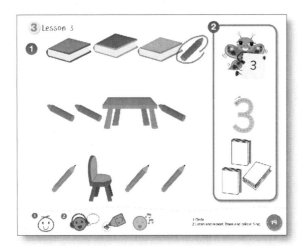

Lesson aims

- To develop cognitive skills by recognising which item is the odd one out.

- To learn the number *3* and become aware of the amount.

Materials: paper napkins (one for each child), a plate of raisins; numbers *1*, *2* and *3* printed on large sheets of paper

Warm up

- Use Horsey to review *pencil, crayon, chair, table, book*. Point to one of the items. Ask *What's this, Horsey?* Make Horsey forget and not be able to say the word. Encourage the children to help Horsey and to call out the words.

1 Circle.

Introduce the activity

- Play the *Odd one out* game with actual items. Put three crayons in a row on a table. Then add a pencil.

- Take Horsey puppet and make him say *Crayon, crayon, crayon …* and then get confused. Make him say *crayon* again and say *No, Horsey! It's a pencil!* Then have Horsey remove the pencil.

- Repeat this with other items, changing the position of the odd one out. Let the children play and remove the odd one out item.

Use the book

- Help the children open their books at page 19.

- Ask what they can see and encourage them to point to the pictures and say the words they remember.

- Now help them to focus on the first row of pictures. Ask if they are all the same. Then ask which one is different (the crayon). Show them that it has been circled. Ask them to take a pencil/crayon and circle the one that is different in the other rows of pictures.

  Answers: Row 1: crayon, Row 2: table, Row 3: chair

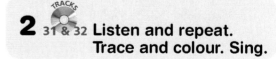 **2** 31 & 32 **Listen and repeat. Trace and colour. Sing.**

Introduce the number *3*

- Hold up the flashcards for numbers *1* and *2* or write those numbers on the board. Say *one, two* as you do so. Now show the flashcard for the number *3* (or write it on the board). Say *three*. Then count all the numbers *one, two, three*. Count on your fingers.

- Now give each child a paper napkin. As you hand them around, say *One for you, one for you, one for you*. Then take a plate of raisins. Go around the class and let each child take three and put them on their napkins. Count with them as they take three raisins.

- See ideas for more number games on pages 22 and 32.

Game Play *Find different numbers.*

- Print the numbers *1*, *2* and *3* on large pieces of paper and put them on tables or the floor. Say the numbers together.

- Then ask the children to find one, two or three of the same item to put on the numbers, e.g. they could put one book on the number 1, two crayons on the number 2 or 3 bags on the number 3.

Use the book

- Show the children that Bella the butterfly is holding another number. Point and say *three*. Hold up three fingers. Point to the books and count them *one, two, three*.

Play the CD

- Play the recording and encourage the children to repeat.

Three [pause] *three* [pause] *three* [pause]

- Help the children to trace the number *3* and colour the three books.

Play the song

- Play the CD and encourage the children to join in.
- The children can hold hands and dance in groups of three as they sing.

One, two, three.
One, two, three.
Look at me!
One, two, three.

Unit 3 Lesson 4

Lesson aims

- To listen to a story which reviews the language of the unit.
- To act out the story.

Materials: a cloth; red tissue paper

Warm up

- Play *What's missing?* Cover a pencil, a book and a crayon with a cloth. Ask the children to cover their eyes. Remove one item. Take off the cloth and encourage the children to call out what is missing. Repeat a few times.

---

1 Listen. Act it out.

- Help the children open their books at page 20.
- Let the children enjoy looking at the pictures for a few moments. Ask them who and what they can see, e.g. Horsey, Jack, Lily, a crayon. Ask what they think Horsey is drawing in picture 2 (his family). Ask what colour Horsey is in picture 4 (red).

Play the CD

- Play the recording several times while the children just listen.

Horsey: *A crayon!*

Horsey: *Me. My mum. My dad.*

Jack and Lily: *Hello, Horsey!*
Horsey: *Hello, Jack. Hello, Lily.*

Lily: *Horsey! You're red!*
Horsey: *Oh!*

 Act it out.

- Use Horsey puppet to act out the scene. Let the children dress up as Jack and Lily. Horsey can pretend to get in a mess with red tissue paper instead of paint. If you have made a *Learning Stars* corner in the classroom, you could act out these scenes in the tent.

Mime the story.

- Play the CD for the story again and show the children how to mime the actions in the story: Horsey pleased to have found a crayon (smile and mime holding up a crayon); Horsey drawing his mum and dad (mime drawing); Jack and Lily coming into the tent and greeting Horsey (mime waving); Horsey realising he is red (point to yourself and make a big 'Oh' with your mouth).

- Do the actions with the children at first, then gradually bow out of the scenes and let them play around with different actions and expressions.

Unit 3 Lesson 5

Lesson aims

- To use the new vocabulary to play a shopping game.

- To learn the sound of the letter *i* and associate it with *insect*.

Materials: shopping lists, a shopping bag, play money, a purse, a shirt; a clean flyswatter; three card circles, tissue paper wings (for each child); a saucer of paint (one for each child) (optional)

Warm up

- Game Play a miming game with the children to review some of the vocabulary they have learnt so far. Pretend to eat an apple. Say *What's this?* and help them to guess. Then pretend to write with a pencil, read a book, sit on a chair, put on a hat or cuddle a doll. See if they can mime actions for these items too.

1 🔘34 **Listen. Play and say.**

Introduce the activity

- 🐴 Put several pencils on a table and ask Horsey to give you one. Say *A pencil, please, Horsey.* Make Horsey say *A pencil!* as he searches for one. As you take it from him, say *Thank you, Horsey.*

- Then play the game with the children. Ask for one pencil, then two, then three.

Use the book

- Help the children open their books at page 21.

- Ask what the children can see in the picture. What do they think the children are doing? (They are playing a shopping game.)

Play the CD

- Play the recording while the children listen.

🔘34 **Girl:** *A pencil, please!*
Boy: *A pencil!*
Girl: *Thank you!*
Girl: *A crayon, please!*
Boy: *A crayon!*
Girl: *Thank you!*
Girl: *A book, please!*
Boy: *A book!*
Girl: *Thank you!*

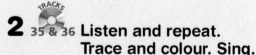 **Act it out.**

- Now make your own shopping lists. Give one child a shopping bag and some play money and a purse. Give another child a shirt to wear to become a shopkeeper. Arrange pencils, books and crayons on a table as if on a shop counter. Help the children to act out the little scene.

- Take the part of the shopkeeper yourself at first. Then swap and let a child be the shopkeeper while you are the customer. Then let two children act out the scene. Repeat so that all the children have a chance to act out the dialogue. You could add numbers too here, e.g. *Two/Three pencils, please.*

2 🔘35 & 36 **Listen and repeat. Trace and colour. Sing.**

Introduce the letter *i*

- 🐴 Show the flashcard of the letter *i* and say the sound /ɪ/. Write the letter on the board and make a point of showing the children that this letter has a little dot above it. You could make Horsey write the dots and make a funny little noise every time he does it.

 44

- Write the letter *i* several times on the board then write other letters from *a–h* around it. First ask Horsey to come and find the *i* letters and then the children.
- See page 20 for more letter games.

Play *Alphabet mosquitoes.*

- Write letters from *a–i* on the board. Draw simple mosquito shapes around them (just a circle with wings would do).
- Give Horsey a clean flyswatter. Ask Horsey to find one of the letters, e.g. say /b/. Make Horsey swat the correct 'mosquito' with the swatter. Then let the children play. The other children could buzz like mosquitoes.
- Now show the flashcard of an insect or draw an insect on the board. All insects have three main body parts, which can be drawn with three circles. As you draw the head, say *one*, then draw the thorax and say *two*, then draw the abdomen and say *three*. Draw wings and six legs. You could count the legs as you draw them too. Do not worry that the children have not learnt numbers up to six yet, they will understand and some of them will pick up on the new numbers. Do not try to teach these new numbers yet. Say *Insect. It's an insect.*

Make insects.

- Give the children three card circles and help them to glue them together to make insects. Give them tissue paper wings and help them to paste them to their insect picture. Then help them to draw six lines for legs and big dots for eyes.

- You could also make fingerprint insects. Give each child a saucer of paint. They dip in one finger and make a mark on the paper. Then they dip again and make another mark touching the first one. The third mark completes the insect's body. Help them add eyes, legs and wings.

Use the book

- Show the children that Horsey has a new letter on his necklace today. Point and say the sound /ɪ/. Point to the insect and say *insect*. Say /ɪ/, /ɪ/, /ɪ/, *insect*.

Play the CD

- Play the recording and encourage the children to repeat.

i insect
i i i i
insect

- Help the children to trace the letter *i* and colour the insect.

Play the song

- Write the letters the children have learnt so far on the board. See if the children can remember how to sing their names. Tell them they are going to learn three more names today *g, h* and *i*.
- Play the CD and encourage the children to join in.
- Let the children come up to the board and point to the letters as they sing.
- See page 25 for Teacher's notes on playing the *Eat the letter* game.

a b c
d e f
g h i

Play *Alphabet games.*

- **Water writing:** You need a chalk blackboard for this game. Dip your finger into a bowl of water and write one of the letters from *a–i* on the board. Encourage the children to call out the sound and the associated word before the letter dries. Then let the children take turns to come up to the board and write another letter for the children to call out the sound and associated word.
- **Invisible ink:** Give each child a piece of paper and put a bowl of lemon juice on each table. Give them a short stick or a cotton bud as a writing implement. Help them write letters using lemon juice as ink. The letters will hardly be visible on the paper. Take the papers to a sunny spot and let them dry. The letters will show up as the lemon juice turns brown.
- See also the ideas for other letter games on page 20.

> Playing writing games encourages creativity. Mistakes in writing letters do not matter – the process of writing is more important at this stage than being correct.

Lesson aims

- To learn about how pencils are made.
- To recognise which things are made from wood.

Materials: several things made from wood, e.g. wooden bricks, a piece of plain, unpainted wood (optional), a picture of a tree; leaves from trees in the playground or surrounding area, tissue paper

Warm up

- 🔘 **16** Sing the *Tidy up* song from Unit 2 and make sure the classroom is neat. As you put crayons, pencils and books away, say their names.

1 Circle.

Introduce the topic

- Have several things which are made from wood to show the children, e.g. wooden bricks, and, if possible a piece of plain, unpainted wood. Say *This is wood.*
- Then show them a picture of a tree, or even better go out and touch a tree in the school playground. Tell them *This is a tree. It's wood. Wood comes from trees.*

Use the book

- Help the children open their books at page 22.
- This lesson teaches the children about things made from wood and where wood comes from. Point out the process in the photos: how trees are cut down, then sawed up and then finally made into other items such as pencils.
- Look at the big picture together and decide which things are made from wood. Help the children colour circles around those items (i.e. the chair, table and bed).
- Look around the classroom. Prompt the children to point to things which are made from wood, e.g. the door, the table, etc.

Nature activity

- Go outside and look at trees together. Show the children that different trees have different leaves. Pick some of the leaves and jumble them up. Can they find the right trees for each leaf?
- Put each leaf between tissue paper and place it within the pages of a book. Place more books on top to add weight. Leave for a week. Your leaf will be pressed.

PE activity

- Do the Tree yoga pose with the children (see teacher's website, http://www.macmillan younglearners.com/learningstars/teacher): stand on one leg with your other leg bent and the foot resting against the straight leg; fold your arms in against your chest and clasp the palms of your hands together. See how long you can hold the pose.

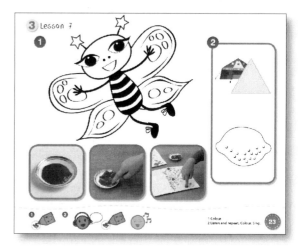

Lesson aims

- To colour a picture of Bella the butterfly using finger paints.
- To learn the colour *yellow* and become familiar with the shape *triangle.*

Materials: pictures of red items, e.g. strawberries, tomatoes and cherries; saucers of finger paints (one for each table), wet and dry towels; red and yellow cards (enough for each child to have either one red card or one yellow card); lemons, a knife; card triangles (one for each child); sandwiches; tomato cards, lemon cards (enough for each child to have either a tomato card or a lemon card)

Warm up

- Draw a square on the board and see if the children can remember the word for it. Now draw a square in the air and get them to do the same. Chant *Square, square, square* as you do so.
- Show the children some pictures of items that are red, e.g. strawberries, tomatoes and cherries. Say *red* and encourage the children to repeat.

 Colour.

Use the book

- Help the children open their books at page 23.
- Colour Bella the butterfly with fingerprints. Give each table of children some saucers of finger paints. Show them how to dip one finger in the paint then press it onto the paper. Have wet and dry towels on the table so that the children can clean their finger before they use another colour.

 **37 & 38 Listen and repeat. Colour. Sing.**

Introduce the colour *yellow*

- Show the children the flashcard for the colour yellow and gather together some items which are yellow: crayons, books, bags, pencils. Point to each one and say *Yellow. A yellow pencil. Yellow. A yellow book.* Now do the same with red items to review that colour.
- Hand out coloured cards: some red ones and some yellow. The children with the red cards

should find one red item in the class. The children with the yellow ones should find and bring you a yellow item.

- Show the flashcard of a lemon and say *lemon.* Take some lemons into the class. Hold one up and say *Lemon. It's a lemon.* Have Horsey say *It's yellow!* Say *Yes, Horsey. It's a yellow lemon. Clever Horsey!*
- Cut up the lemons, remove the pips and give them to the children to suck. Young children often enjoy the sharp taste of lemons.

Introduce the shape *triangle*

- Show the flashcard of the triangle shape and say *triangle.* Draw a triangle on the board and count the sides as you do so *one, two, three.* Draw another triangle and do the same. Make some large, some small, some with equal sides and some with unequal sides. Each time say *Triangle. It's a triangle.* and count the sides as you draw.
- Demonstrate the Triangle yoga pose (see teacher's website) and encourage the children to join in.

Game Play *Triangle games.*

- Draw a house with a triangular roof on the board. Ask children to come up to the front and point to the triangle in your drawing. Give the children card triangles and help them draw around them to make roofs then complete the house beneath it.
- Pizza shapes are almost triangular too – you could have a class picnic and look at the shapes of different foods.

Use the book

- Point to the yellow triangle. Say *yellow.* Draw a triangle with your finger and say *triangle.* Say *A yellow triangle.*

- Ask the children to open their books at page 3 and see if they can find the same shape on the rug.
- Point to the lemon and say *lemon.*

Play the CD

- Play the recording and encourage the children to repeat.

 37 *Yellow, yellow, yellow Lemon! Lemon!*

- Help the children to colour the lemon yellow. Ask them if they can think of other natural things which are yellow, e.g. a banana.
- Have them look and point to things which are triangles in the classroom.

Play the song

- Play the CD and encourage the children to join in.

38 *Yellow, yellow, yellow, Yellow, yellow, yellow, Lemon! Lemon! Yellow, yellow, yellow.*

Do a colour dance

- **24 & 38** Sing the two colour songs (the *Red tomato* song from Unit 2 and the *Yellow lemon* song from Unit 3). Give half the class tomato cards and the other half lemon ones. They hold up their cards when they hear their colour.
- You could make this into a class dance with the children in a circle. They skip into the centre when they hear their colour.

Unit 4 Toys

By the end of Unit 4 the children will be able to:

- say the words for toys: *kite, ball, teddy, train, doll.*
- perform the classroom routine of putting rubbish in the bin and recognise which items are rubbish and which are not.
- say the sounds, sing the names and trace the letters *j, k* and *l.*
- recognise that *jelly* goes with *j, kite* with *k* and *lemon* with *l.*
- recognise and say the number *4* and understand the amount.
- understand which things move and which do not.
- recognise and say the colour *green* and be aware of the shape *circle.*
- make a puzzle.

New/Reviewed words and language

kite, ball, teddy, train, doll
/dʒ/, /k/, /l/, *j, k, l*
jelly, kite, lemon
4, four
move
green, circle, leaf

Classroom language

Come with me.
I've got a (teddy).
Put the rubbish in the bin, please.
Thank you.
Where's (Teddy)?
Colour the (leaf).
Stop!

Value of the unit

I put rubbish in the bin.

Materials

paper, scissors, a hole punch, crayons, pencils, glue, card
Horsey puppet
flashcards
CD

Unit 4 Lesson 1

Lesson aims

- To learn/review and say the words: *kite, ball, teddy, train, doll.*
- To learn the sound of the letter *j* and associate it with *jelly.*

Materials: a cardboard box, clean, shredded wastepaper, toys: a ball, a car, a train, a doll; a teddy, a toy kite, a diamond shaped piece of card, string, tissue paper (optional), a bag; several dolls, trains, balls, teddies and card kites (optional); a tambourine or music; an apron for each child, a packet of jelly, boiling water, cold water, a bowl and spoon, little plastic bowls and spoons; white wax crayon, white paper, paint, paintbrushes (one for each child); wooden spoons (one for each child), marker pens, pieces of wool, cut-outs of clothes from coloured card (see teacher's website)

Warm up

- 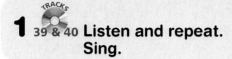 Fill a cardboard box with clean, shredded wastepaper. Add toys: a ball, a car, a train and a doll. Let the children come up to the front one by one and feel around for a toy in the box. Before they pull it out, encourage them to guess what they have found. Say the word as they pull it out. Then they put it back in again and another child has a go.

1 39 & 40 **Listen and repeat. Sing.**

Introduce the vocabulary

- Take toys into the classroom: a train, a ball, a doll, a teddy and a kite. If you do not have a kite, make a small one from a diamond shaped piece of card and add a string tail decorated with tissue paper bows. Put them all in a bag and take them out, one by one saying the word as you do so.

- Give the children flashcards of the toys and get them to put their card next to the correct toy.

- If possible, have several dolls, trains, balls, teddies and card kites. Let the children choose which one they would like on their desk.

- Now bang a tambourine or play music. Stop and call out *Doll!* All the children who have dolls on their desks, stand up and hold up the toy. You could do this in a circle too, i.e. the children hold their toys and dance around in a circle; when you call out the name of a toy, the children holding it dance into the centre of the circle.

Use the book

- Help the children open their books at page 24.

- Ask the children to point and say the names of the characters in the picture (Jack, Lily, Horsey and Bella).

Play the CD

- Play the recording and encourage the children to repeat.

kite
ball
teddy
train
doll

- Point out the ball's bouncy path and help the children to trace over this pre-writing line.

- Prompt the children to name the toys. Say *Look at Bella. What has she got? A kite!* Then ask the question again without supplying the answer. Do the same for the other characters.

Play the song

- Play the CD and encourage the children to join in.

- Sing the song again and hold up flashcards or real toys as you sing. When it comes to the bit about the train, all line up, hold on to each other and dance and sing around the classroom making 'chuff, chuff' train noises.

I've got a teddy, I've got a doll,
I've got a ball and a kite.
I've got a train.
Come with me.
[repeat]
One two three, one two three,
one two three, come with me!
Chuff chuff chuff, chuff chuff chuff,
chuff chuff chuff,
Come with me!

2 41 **Listen and repeat. Trace and colour.**

Introduce the letter *j*

- 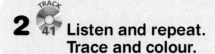 Show the flashcard of the letter *j* and say the sound. Write it on the board several times, saying the sound each time. Let Horsey make a funny noise every time you add the dot above the letter. Then add other letters from *a–i* on the board and get Horsey to point to the *j* letters. Then let the children do the same.

- Show the flashcard of jelly and say *Jelly. It's a jelly.* Pretend to wobble like a jelly and encourage the children to do the same. You could put on some music and all do a wobbly jelly dance.

- See pages 20 and 45 for more letter games.

Cookery activity

- All wash your hands and put on aprons. Get a packet of jelly and make it with the children, according to the instructions. Make sure they stand clear when you are adding the boiling water, but let them add the cold water.

Let them stir the jelly mixture until it has dissolved. Take the children with you while you put the jelly in the fridge and then tell them you must all be patient and wait until tomorrow to eat the jelly.

- Take in little plastic bowls and spoons and enjoy the jelly the following day. Remind them that if they make jelly at home, they must always have help from Mummy or Daddy with the hot water.

 Make magic letters.

- Write the letter *j* with a white wax crayon on white paper.
- Give the children some paint and a paintbrush and show them how to paint over the letter. The paint will not be absorbed on the wax and the letter will be revealed. If they enjoy doing this, encourage them to ask for other letters. Help them to say the sounds of the letters.

 Make dolls.

- Give the children a wooden spoon each (see teacher's website, http://www.macmillan younglearners.com/learning stars/teacher). Help them to draw faces on their spoons and stick on wool for hair. Cut clothes for the children from coloured card. Let the children choose how they wish to dress their dolls and help them to stick the clothes onto the handles of their spoons.

Use the book

- Point to the picture of Horsey. Say that he has a new letter on his necklace today. Point and say the sound /dʒ/. Point to the jelly and say *jelly*. Say /dʒ/, /dʒ/, /dʒ/, *jelly*.

Play the CD

- Play the recording and encourage the children to repeat.

j jelly
j j j j
jelly

- Help the children to trace the letter *j* and colour the jelly.

Unit 4 Lesson 2

Lesson aims

- To become familiar with the classroom routine of putting rubbish in the bin.
- To become aware of what is and what is not rubbish.
- To learn the sound of the letter *k* and associate it with *kite*.

Materials: a tambourine or drum (optional); (clean) rubbish items, e.g. torn paper, used cartons, pencil shavings, a doll; scrap paper, ribbon; scraps of old paper (one piece for each child); chalk, small watering cans or plastic tumblers filled with water

Warm up

- 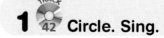 Play a jumping game to review the numbers *1–3*. Call out *one* and get the children to jump once, then stop. Then call out *two* and they jump twice. Call out *three* and they jump three times. Do this a couple of times so that they get the idea and then call out the numbers in random order. You could beat a tambourine or bang a drum and get them to call out the number of beats as they jump.

1 🔊42 **Circle. Sing.**

Introduce the routine

- Put some (clean) rubbish items on the table, e.g. torn paper, used cartons, pencil shavings. Point and say *Rubbish. This is rubbish.* Now add some things which are not rubbish, e.g. a doll, a book, a pencil. Ask *Horsey, rubbish? Is this rubbish, Horsey?* Make Horsey say *No!* and put them to one side.
- Then point to the bin and say *Put the rubbish in the bin, please, Horsey.* Make Horsey take one item of rubbish and put it in the bin. Say *Good, Horsey, thank you!* Do this a few times and then ask the children to put some rubbish in the bin.

Make recycled notebooks.

- Help the children become aware of recycling by using scrap paper to make notebooks. Show them that instead of throwing away a piece of paper which is only partially drawn upon, you are salvaging the clean part. Cut scraps into the same shape and size, punch holes and tie with ribbons for the children to reuse.

Use the book

- Help the children open their books at page 25.
- Look at the pictures together. Ask the children which items they think are rubbish. Then ask if the pencil is rubbish and if they should throw that in the bin? Help the children to circle the items which should be thrown away (the apple core, the used drink carton, the banana skin, the torn paper).

Play the song

- Play the CD and encourage the children to join in.
- Put a rubbish bin in the centre of the classroom. Give each child a scrap of old paper.
- Play the song several times and prompt the children to take turns to put the scraps of paper in the bin as they sing.

 Put the rubbish in the bin
Put the rubbish in the bin
Put the rubbish in the bin, please.
Thank you!

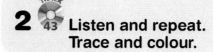
2 Listen and repeat. Trace and colour.

Introduce the letter k

- Show the flashcard of the letter *k* and say the sound. Write it several times on the board, saying the sound each time. Write other letters around it and then get Horsey and the children to find the *k* letters.
- See pages 20 and 45 for more letter games.

 Play *Disappearing letters.*

- In the school playground, write the letters from *a–k* in chalk. Space the letters wide apart from each other. Draw a simple flower shape around each letter. Give the children small watering cans or plastic tumblers of water. Say the sound of a letter and the children water that letter until it disappears.

Use the book

- Show the children that Horsey has a new letter on his necklace. Point and say the sound /k/. Point to the kite and prompt them to say the word. Then say /k/, /k/, /k/, *kite*.

Play the CD

- Play the recording and encourage the children to repeat.

 k kite
k k k k
kite

- Help the children to trace the letter *k* and colour the kite.

When possible, use good quality paper and art supplies for the children's art and craft work. Some of them may still only be scribbling at this stage, but having nice paper to do it on gives the activity more value and encourages them to do better drawings and writing.

Unit 4 Lesson 3

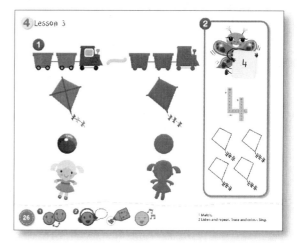

Lesson aims

- To match pictures of toys to their shapes.
- To learn the number *4* and become aware of the amount.

Materials: wrapping paper or dark tissue paper, a doll; paper plates (a set of four plates for each table), fruit on a platter (one for each table), a knife; four boxes, soft balls or beanbags

Warm up

- Mime playing with a doll, train, car and ball, e.g. throw an imaginary ball in the air and pretend to catch it, rock an imaginary doll to sleep, make driving a car noises and chuff like a train. Encourage the children to call out the names of the toys. Then help the children to take turns to do the mimes.

1 Match.

Introduce the activity

- Wrap some items in wrapping paper, e.g. a pencil, a doll, a book. The shape of the object should still be clear so it might be best to use dark tissue paper which is more pliable.
- Put them on the table and say *Where's the doll?* Let children come and pick up the correct item.
- Now give them some wrapping paper and help them to wrap something, e.g. a small toy or school item. They give their wrapped item to their friend to guess what it is.

Use the book

- Help the children open their books at page 26.
- Encourage the children to point to the pictures and say which toys they can see (train, kite, ball, doll).
- Then draw their attention to the shapes on the right and show them the example. Ask them if they can find the correct shape for each toy. Help them to trace over the sample line; then draw short lines to match the other toys to the correct shapes.

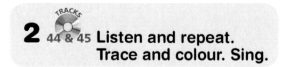

2 44 & 45 Listen and repeat. Trace and colour. Sing.

Introduce the number 4

- Show the flashcard for the number *4* or write the number on the board and say *four.* Now put four of the same item on a table (four books, four crayons) and count them as you put them down *One, two, three, four.*
- See ideas for more number games on pages 22 and 32.

Game Play *Put it on the plate.*

- Write numbers *1, 2, 3* and *4* on paper plates. Put a set of four plates on each table.
- Get everyone to wash their hands and dry them. Wash some fruit and cut it up into small pieces. Place a platter of fruit on each table. The children have to put one piece of fruit on the plate marked 1, two pieces on the plate marked 2 and so on. When they have put the correct amounts on each plate, let them eat the pieces of fruit. (If some children eat more than others, hand out more pieces of fruit, counting them as you do so.)

Use the book

- Show the children that Bella has a new number today. Point and say *four.* Hold up four fingers as you do so. Point to the kites and count them, *One, two, three, four. Four kites.*

Play the CD

- Play the recording and encourage the children to repeat.

Four [pause] *four* [pause] *four* [pause]

- Help the children to trace the number *4* and colour the kites.

Play the song

- Play the CD and encourage the children to join in.
- Sing the song again and do the actions: the children skip around the classroom then sit down when they get to the last line.

1 2 3 4
Skip with me, skip, skip, skip
1 2 3 4
Skip with me then sit, sit, sit!

Game Play *Throw the ball.*

- Label four boxes with the numbers *1–4.* Give the children soft balls or beanbags. Call out one of the numbers and they throw a ball into the correct box. Then let the children call out the numbers. You could ask them to throw one ball into the box marked 1, two into the box marked 2 and so on.

Lesson aims

- To listen to a story which reviews the language of the unit.
- To act out the story.

Materials: real toys for props

Warm up

- Play a *No, thank you!* game with Horsey puppet. Make Horsey look as if he needs cheering up, i.e. sit him down with his head hung low. Offer him a toy. Make him look at you then shake his head and politely say *No, thank you.* Repeat this with other toys. Finally, offer him a book and make Horsey jump up, act happy and say *Thank you!*

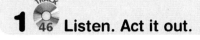
1 46 Listen. Act it out.

- Help the children open their books at page 27.
- Let them have a few moments to look at the pictures. Ask them who they can see and what toys there are. Then ask why they think Jack is looking sad.

Play the CD

- Play the recording several times while the children just listen.
- When the children have heard the complete story, play it again pausing after each frame to ask questions in L1, e.g. What does Jack want? What toy has Lily/Bella got? What toy has Horsey got? Is Jack happy now?

TRACK 46

Jack: *Where's Teddy?*
Lily: *Look, Jack, a car!*
Jack: *No, thank you.*

Jack: *Where's Teddy?*
Lily: *Look, Jack, a train!*
Jack: *No, thank you!*

Jack: *Where's Teddy?*
Bella: *Look, Jack, a kite!*
Jack: *No, thank you.*

Horsey: *Look, Jack – Teddy!*
Jack: *Thank you, Horsey!*

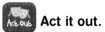 Act it out.

- Let the children dress up as Lily, Bella and Jack and use Horsey puppet to act out this story. Use real toys as props (you could add more scenes with other toys). In the story, the teddy is in a tree; let the children decide on different places to hide teddy.
- Prepare for the dramatic play first. In the story, Jack is sad when he cannot find his teddy. Play around with different expressions of sadness. Ask questions in L1, e.g. Do the children cry when they are sad? Do they go quiet? What about when they are happy? Do they always laugh? Or do they just feel happy inside. Can they remember when they last felt sad or happy? What made them feel like that?

> **Tip** Playing simple acting games about our emotions helps our children to express themselves more freely when they are at school. They might not want to admit to feeling sad at school sometimes and drama and role-play can help us all understand each other better.

Lesson aims

- To play a guessing game with toys.
- To learn the sound of the letter *l* and associate it with *lemon*.

Materials: a cushion; toys; a pack of small envelopes, small pieces of card, glue sticks, glitter; plastic letters (two of each letter *a–l*), small pieces of card (optional), 24 plastic cups (see teacher's website)

Warm up

- Game Play *Jump and Say.* Put a cushion on the floor and ask the children to jump over it. Then stand next to the cushion and hold up a flashcard of something they have already learnt. As they jump, the children say the word. If they cannot remember, tell them the word and show them the same flashcard next time it is their turn.

1 Play and say.

Introduce the activity

- Hide toys around the room. Say *Where's Teddy?* and encourage the children to search for him. Say *Here he is!* when you find him. Do the same with the doll *Where's Dolly? Here she is!*

Use the book

- Help the children open their books at page 28.
- Ask the children what is happening in the picture (the children are playing a game). Then ask what they think is happening in the game. Ask who has got the teddy. Let them point to the correct child in the picture. Now tell them they are going to play the same game. Let them decide which toy they want to use.
- Three children line up. Another child stands with his or her back to them. Give the toy to one of the children to hold behind their back. The other child turns around and guesses who is holding it.

2 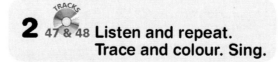 47 & 48 Listen and repeat. Trace and colour. Sing.

Introduce the letter *l*

- Show the flashcard of the letter *l* and say the sound. Write it on the board several times, saying the sound each time. Show the children that this is a nice easy letter to write. Let them come and try to write it on the board too.
- See pages 20 and 45 for more letter games.

Game Play *Alphabet envelopes.*

- Take a pack of small envelopes and write the letters *a–l* on the front – one letter on each envelope. Now give the children small cards with the letters printed on them. Help them to trace over the letters with a glue stick and then shake glitter on them. When they are dry, they put the letters into the correct envelopes.

Use the book

- Show the children that Horsey has a new letter on his necklace today. Point and say the sound /l/. Point to the lemon and ask if they can remember the word *lemon* and what colour it is. Say *Lemon. /l/, /l/, /l/, lemon.*

Play the CD

- Play the recording and encourage the children to repeat.

TRACK
47

l lemon
l l l l
lemon

- Help the children to trace the letter *l* and colour the lemon.

Play the song

- Remind the children that letters have names as well as sounds. Ask them if they can remember the *Alphabet* song so far.
- Play the CD and encourage the children to join in.
- Write the letters on the board and have the children point to them as they sing again. Alternatively, give out the alphabet flashcards and the children hold them up.

- See page 25 for Teacher's notes on playing the *Eat the letter* game.

TRACK 48
a b c
d e f
g h i
j k l
[repeat]

Game Play *Match the letters.*

- Place plastic letters from *a–l* on a table. You need two of each letter. If you do not have toy letters, write them on small cards. Place them in random order and cover each one with a plastic cup (see teacher's website, http://www.macmillanyounglearners.com/learningstars/teacher).

- One child removes one cup then tries to find its pair by removing another cup. If the letters match, the cups stay off. If they do not, put the cups back in place. The next child now has a turn.

> **Tip** Play around with language. You can call the doll *Dolly*, teddy can be *Ted* or *Big Ted* or *Little Ted*. This will help the children to feel free and natural when they speak English.

Unit 4 Lesson 6

Lesson aim

- To think about movement and which things can move.

Materials: toy cars, boxes; music; a toy train, a picture of a house; plastic drinking straws

Warm up

- **16 & 42** Tidy up the classroom before you start. Sing the *Tidy up* song and the *Put the rubbish in the bin* song.

1 Colour.

Introduce the topic

- Put some toy cars on the floor. Say *car* as you put each one down. Make bridges from boxes and let the children have fun trying to push the cars so that they go under them. Say *The cars are moving!* as they play.

Game Play *Musical statues.*

- Play some music and let the children dance and move around the classroom. Say *Move, move, move* as they dance. When you pause the music, they have to stop and stand still like a statue. Say *Stop! Stop moving.*

Use the book

- Help the children open their books at page 29.

- Point to the three photos at the top of the page: the train, a child running and a car. Take a toy car and make it move. Say *Look, it's moving.* Ask one of the children to run. Say *Look, he/she's moving.* Take a toy train and make it move and repeat the phrase, *Look, it's moving.* Make the train stop. Say *It isn't moving.* Then make it move again until they understand what you are showing them.

- Show them a house and ask *Do houses move?* Shake your head and answer *No.*

- Now look at the main picture and the other photos and decide together what is moving. Ask them to colour the stars next to the objects which move: the mother and child, the car, the boat, the train and the bus.

Science activities

- Put a book on the table and ask the children to push it. Then place some plastic drinking straws under the book. Ask them to push it again. Is it easier this time? Explain that the straws help the book to roll and it is easier to roll something than to slide it.

- Give the children toy cars. Put one upside down on your table. Push it and show that it does not move easily. Turn it onto its wheels. Push it again and show that the wheels make it easier.

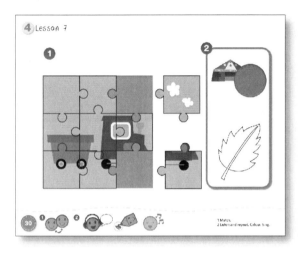

Lesson aims

- To develop cognitive skills by completing a puzzle.
- To make a simple puzzle.
- To learn the colour *green* and become familiar with the shape *circle*.

Materials: picture of a car or a toy car; wooden jigsaw puzzles with four pieces; printed flashcards (one for each table) (see teacher's website); items which are green, e.g. green toy cars, red or yellow items, a worksheet of naturally green items, e.g. a leaf, a cucumber, a pepper (one for each child) (optional), pots of green crayons; saucers of blue paint, saucers of yellow paint, clean saucers, paintbrushes; photocopy of a simple flower (one for each child to colour), pots of red crayons, pots of yellow crayons, circular cards; a hula hoop, masking tape, music; pictures of cars, slices of tomato or cucumber (optional)

Warm up

- Play a moving game. Show the children flashcards of a cat, a goat, an insect, a train and a picture of a car or a toy car. Help them to remember the words.
- Say *Move like a cat.* Make cat movements and encourage the children to join in. Then say *Stop!* Then say *Move like a car.* and let the children pretend to be driving around the classroom. Continue with the other items.
- Demonstrate the Train yoga pose (see teacher's website) and encourage the children to join in.

1 Match.

Introduce the activity

- Play with Horsey puppet and simple wooden jigsaw puzzles which have four pieces. Make Horsey try to put the puzzle together and get it wrong. Let the children call out *Yes* or *No* as he tries to put the pieces in the correct place. Then let them help him get it right.

Use the book

- Help the children open their books at page 30.
- Look at the puzzle together. Ask them what they think the finished puzzle will show (a train). Point out that two pieces are missing and draw attention to the missing pieces on the right.
- Give them time to work out which piece goes where and point to the correct spaces. Then help them draw matching lines from the pieces to the spaces.

Make a puzzle.

- Download flashcards from the teacher's website, http://www.macmillanyounglearners.com/learningstars/teacher. Give a picture to each table and help them to glue their picture onto a sheet of card.
- Cut the pictures into four pieces for them, then hand these out to each group.
- See if they can fit the pieces together to make the picture complete. Groups can then swap puzzles with each other.

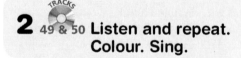

2 49 & 50 Listen and repeat. Colour. Sing.

Introduce the colour *green*

- Show the flashcard for the colour green and gather together items which are green, e.g. pencils, crayons, books, toy cars. Say *Green. A green car. Green. A green crayon.* as you put them on a table.
- Now add one yellow item. Ask Horsey *Is it green?* Make Horsey say *No!* Say *That's right, Horsey. It isn't green. It's yellow!*
- Now play odd one out with three green items and one red or yellow item. Get the children to take away the odd item. Encourage them to say the colours as they do so.
- Draw outlines of three things which are naturally green, e.g. a leaf, a cucumber and a pepper. You could make this into a worksheet by drawing in black pen on white paper and photocopying it. Put pots of green crayons on the table and let the children colour the items.

Make green paint.

- Give the children saucers of blue paint, saucers of yellow and a clean saucer. Show them how to take a little blue paint on their paintbrush and put it on the clean saucer. Then they wash their brushes and add some yellow paint to the blue. They mix it up and say *green*.

 Play *Colour by numbers.*

- Draw a simple flower with petals, a centre and a stem and leaves. Write *1* on each petal, *2* in the centre and *3* on the stem and leaves. Photocopy it so that each child has one.

- Place pots of red crayons next to a card with the number 1 on it, a pot of yellow crayons next to a card with the number 2 and a pot of green crayons next to the number 3. Help the children to colour their flowers according to the code.

Introduce the shape *circle*

- Show the flashcard of the circle shape and say *circle*. Hold up a circular piece of white card and say *Circle. It's a circle*. Draw a circle on the board and say *circle*. Give the children circular cards to draw around.

 Play *Jump into the shapes.*

- Put a hula hoop on the floor. Say *Jump into the circle.* and let the children take turns to jump into it. Now use masking tape to make a triangle on the floor too. Make them large so that several children can stand in the shapes together. Play some music and let them dance around the shapes. When you stop the music call out *Triangle!* or *Circle!* and they jump into the correct shape. Then add a square shape.

Use the book

- Point to the green circle. Say *green*. Draw a circle with your finger and say *circle*. Say *A green circle*.

- Ask the children to open their books at page 3 and see if they can find the same shape on the rug.

- Point to the leaf and say *leaf*. Show the flashcard of a leaf and say *leaf*.

Play the CD

- Play the recording and encourage the children to repeat.

Green, green, green
Leaf! Leaf!

- Help the children to colour the leaf green. Ask the children to name other natural things which are green, e.g. apple, grass, green pepper.

- Have the children look and point to things that are circles in the classroom. Show pictures of cars and ask them to identify the circles there. You could also hold up slices of tomato or cucumber, etc.

Play the song

- Play the CD and encourage the children to join in.

Green, green, green,
Green, green, green,
Leaf! Leaf!
Green, green, green.

Lesson aim

- To review the main vocabulary of Units 3 and 4.

Warm up

- If you made your own puzzles in the previous lesson, put the completed puzzles on the table and let the children choose which one they would like to play with. Hand them out and let them take them apart and put them together again. They might like to only play with the ones they have made themselves, but try to encourage sharing.

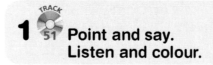

1 TRACK **51** Point and say.
Listen and colour.

Introduce the activity

- Put two flashcards on the board: one of a ball and one of a chair. Draw a star outline next to each of them.

- Say *ball, ball*. Let individual children come up to the front and point to the correct card. Now give one child a coloured marker or coloured chalk and let him or her colour the star next to the picture of the ball. Now say *chair, chair* and let a child colour the star next to the chair. Add other cards of items the children are familiar with.

Use the book

- Help the children open their books at pages 31 and 32.

- Let the children have a few moments to look at the pages and say what they can see.

- Then ask individual children to point to each picture and say the word. Point to pictures in random order so that you can ascertain if they are all familiar with the vocabulary.

Play the CD

- Play the recording and encourage the children to listen.

- Play the CD again. Pause after each word to give the children time to find the matching picture. They then colour the star next to it. Tell the children that if they cannot see the picture on the first page, they will have to turn the page over to look at the pictures on the second page.

TRACK **51**
ball
chair
pencil
crayon
teddy
book

- **Game** Place flashcards of the above items around the classroom. Play the recording again and encourage the children to go to the correct one.

Unit 5 Animals

By the end of Unit 5 the children will be able to:

- say the animal words: *cat, hen, rabbit, bird.*
- perform the classroom routine of putting away their books and differentiate between big and small books and where they go.
- say the sounds, sing the names and trace the letters *m, n, o* and *p.*
- recognise that *mouse* goes with *m*, *nest* with *n*, *orange* with *o* and *pizza* with *p.*
- recognise and say the numbers 5 and 6 and understand the amounts.
- recognise that some animals are awake at night: *owl, bat* and *fox.*
- recognise and say the colour *blue* and be aware of the shape *rectangle.*
- help make animal masks for themselves.

New/Reviewed words and language

cat, hen, rabbit, bird
big, small
/m/, /n/, /ɒ/, /p/, *m, n, o, p*
mouse, nest, orange, pizza
5, five, 6, six
day, night, owl, bat, fox
blue, rectangle, sky

Classroom language

Stop! Go!
Look at the (birds).
Do you like the (cat)?
Good morning. Goodnight.
Put your books away, please.
Colour the (birds).

Value of the unit

I'm kind to animals.

Materials

glue, paper, pencils, crayons, card, scissors, paints
Horsey puppet
flashcards
CD

Unit 5 Lesson 1

Lesson aims

- To learn/review and say the words: *cat, hen, rabbit, bird.*
- To learn the sound of the letter *m* and associate it with *mouse.*

Materials: two large card circles, one green and one red, toy cars; a drum (optional); one large and one small paper triangle, two small circles (for each child) (see teacher's website)

Warm up

- 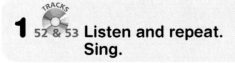 Play a *Stop and Go* game. Cut two large circles, one from red card and one from green. Hold up the green card and say *Go!* Let the children dance or skip around the classroom, or the playground if possible. Then hold up the red card and say *Stop!* The children stop moving. You could demonstrate this game with Horsey first to establish the rules.

- Play this game with toy cars too. Hold up the green card and the children make the cars move. Then hold up the red card and they must make the cars stop.

1 52 & 53 Listen and repeat. Sing.

Introduce the vocabulary

- Use the flashcards of the cat, bird, hen and rabbit. Hold them up one by one and say the words clearly. Say *Cat. Look at the cat.* Put them on a table in a row. Point and say the words again with the children. Now ask the children to close their eyes. Turn one card face down. Ask them to open their eyes and see if they can name the card. When they have understood the game, swap roles and let the children turn over a card for you to guess.

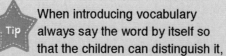

Tip When introducing vocabulary always say the word by itself so that the children can distinguish it, but then feel free to use it in more complex sentences, e.g. *This is a cat. It's a cat. Do you like the cat?* Do not worry that the children cannot fully understand these sentences. This is how children start to feel comfortable in an English-speaking environment. It 'acclimatises' them to the language.

Use the book

- Help the children open their books at page 33.

- Draw attention to the main picture. Ask the children who they can see (Bella, Horsey, Jack and Lily). Point to each animal and say the word clearly.

- Then point to the photos above. Help the children to find the photos which match the pictures of the animals and to say the words.

Play the CD

- Play the recording and encourage the children to repeat.

52

cat
hen
rabbit
bird

Play *Rabbit hops.*

- Show the children how to hop like rabbits (i.e. on two feet together). Let them have fun hopping around the classroom. You could ask them to stand in a big circle and hop in one direction. Then bang a drum, give them time to turn around and they hop the other way.

Play the song

- Play the CD and encourage the children to join in.

- Do simple actions for each animal as you sing: hold your hands up like paws for a cat, nod your head as if clucking like a hen, flap your arms like wings for a bird and hop like a rabbit.

- Play the song several times until all the children are joining in with the words and the actions.

53

Look at the animals!
Look at the animals!
Look at the animals!
Look at the animals – look at them!
Look at the cat and the hen
A bird and a rabbit – hop hop hop
Look at all the animals in the shop!
Look at the animals!

2 54 Listen and repeat. Trace and colour.

Introduce the letter *m*

- Show the flashcard of the letter *m* and say the sound. Write it on the board several times, saying the sound each time. Add other letters to the board and let Horsey and then the children come and point to the *m* letters.

- Show the flashcard of a mouse and say *Mouse*. /m/ *mouse*.

- Put flashcards with the letters *a–m* on one table and flashcards with the alphabet pictures (apple, ball, cat, etc.) on another. Let the children play in pairs or groups of three to match the pictures and the letters, and bring them to you and Horsey.

- See pages 20 and 45 for more letter games.

Craft Make a triangle mouse.

- Give each child one large and one small paper triangle. Help them to remember the word *triangle*. Give them two small circles and help them to remember the word *circle*.

- Show them how to stick the triangles together to make simple mice, e.g. place the larger triangle on a sheet of paper with the point facing upwards. Place the smaller triangle at the top at a slight angle. Stick the circles to the points of the smaller triangle for ears. Help them to draw whiskers, legs, a tail, eyes and a black nose (see teacher's website, http://www.macmillanyounglearners.com/learningstars/teacher).

Tip The plural of *mouse* is the irregular *mice*, but for children it is just another word. They might have got the idea of making plurals by adding an *s* so if they say *mouses* just agree with them and say *Yes, mice*, without mentioning that *mouses* is incorrect.

Use the book

- Show the children that Horsey has a new letter on his necklace. Point and say the sound /m/. Point to the mouse and say *mouse*. Say /m/, /m/, /m/, *mouse*.

Play the CD

- Play the recording and encourage the children to repeat.

TRACK 54

m mouse

m m m m

mouse

- Help the children to trace the letter *m* and colour the mouse.

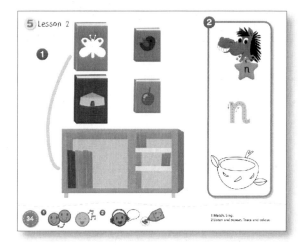

Unit 5 Lesson 2

Lesson aims

- To become familiar with the classroom routine of putting books on the bookshelf.

- To differentiate between big and small books and where they should go.

- To learn the sound of the letter *n* and associate it with *nest*.

Materials: paper plates (one for each child); big and small teddies or dolls, two boxes or bags, one big and one small; paper plates (one for each child), brown paint, a paintbrush for each child, oval bird shapes (one for each child), torn strips of yellow and brown paper or real straw or dried grass (see teacher's website)

Warm up

- 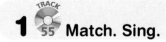 Play a carrying game. Give each child a paper plate. Place one crayon on each and let them carry it from one end of the class to the other. Now add a pencil and let them carry it again. Keep adding more small (unbreakable) items so that they have to keep the plate steady as they walk and not drop anything.

1 🔲55 Match. Sing.

Introduce the routine

- Gather together some large items (e.g. school bags, large books, big teddies or dolls) and some smaller ones (e.g. crayons, rubbers, pencils). Have two boxes or bags ready – one big and one small. Hold up one of the big items.

- Say *Teddy. Big Teddy!* Ask Horsey where you should put it. Have Horsey try to put it in the small box/bag. Laugh and say *No, Horsey. Look, small box/bag.*

- Then let the children show Horsey where the big teddy will fit and say *Yes, Horsey. Big box/bag.*

- Do the same with the other items. Say *Yes, big book, big box/bag* as the children place them in the correct box/bag.

Use the book

- Help the children open their books at page 34.

- Point to the picture and see if they can remember the word *book.*

- Ask them to point to the big books. Ask them where they think they should go in the shelf below. Encourage them to point to the correct place. Do the same with the small books.

- Help them to trace over the sample line; then ask them to draw a matching line from the second big book to the large space on the bookshelf and from the small books to the small spaces.

Play the song

- Play the CD and encourage the children to join in.

- Place big books around the classroom and let the children pick them up and place them in the correct place (i.e. on a large shelf) as they sing.

- Then sing the song again and this time place small books around the classroom.

- Eventually, mix up the books so that the children have to decide which books go where.

🔲55

Put your books away, please.
Put your books away!
Big books, small books,
small books, big books,
Put your books away!
[repeat]

---

2 🔲56 Listen and repeat. Trace and colour.

Introduce the letter *n*

- Show the flashcard of the letter *n* and say the sound. Write it on the board several times, saying the sound each time. Let the children come up to the board and trace over the letters with a different coloured marker or piece of chalk.

- Show the flashcard of a nest and say *Nest.* /n/ *nest.*

- See pages 20 and 45 for more letter games.

🔲 Play *Guess the picture.*

- Place several alphabet picture flashcards on a table.

- Take a piece of blank card and cut a hole in it. Place it over one of the pictures. Only a small part of the picture will be visible through the hole. Encourage the children to say the word. You can move the card around so that the children see different parts of the picture until they are able to guess what it is.

Use the book

- Show the children that Horsey has a new letter on his necklace. Point and say the sound for the letter *n.* Point to the nest and say *nest.* Say /n/, /n/, /n/, *nest.*

Play the CD

- Play the recording and encourage the children to repeat.

n nest

n n n n

nest

- Help the children to trace the letter *n* and colour the nest.

 Craft Make a hen's nest.

- Take paper plates and fold them in half. Give the children brown paint and let them paint their plates. When they are dry, glue the sides together, leaving an opening at the top. In the meantime, give the children oval bird shapes and help them to draw eyes and beaks on them. Place the painted birds in the nests. Add torn strips of yellow and brown paper for straw or add some real straw or dried grass to the nests (see teacher's website, http://www.macmillanyounglearners.com/learningstars/teacher).

Unit 5 Lesson 3

Lesson aims

- To develop cognitive skills by doing a sequencing activity which practises the animal vocabulary and colours.
- To learn the numbers *5* and *6* and become aware of the amounts.

Materials: pencil outlines of a hen, cat, bird or rabbit on paper towels, water, paints and paintbrushes for each child

Warm up

- **Craft** Draw pencil outlines of a hen, cat, bird or rabbit on paper towels. Give the children water, paints and paintbrushes and let them have fun colouring in the animals. Because the towels absorb the paint, the effects are different to what they would be on normal paper. Ask if the children think the cats and rabbits look fluffier and if the birds look more feathery.

1 Colour.

Introduce the activity

- Gather together items which are the same but are different colours, e.g. some red and yellow crayons. Place them in a simple sequence of colours on a table: one red crayon, one yellow crayon, one red, one yellow. Point to them with the children and say the colours together: *red, yellow, red, yellow*.
- Now put a red and yellow crayon on the table. Ask which colour crayon they should put down to continue the sequence (the red one). Let them choose and put the crayon in place. Repeat this a few times.

Use the book

- Help the children open their books at page 35.
- Draw their attention to the top row and elicit the name of the animal, *cat*. Ask them which colour comes next in each sequence. Help the children to identify the pattern and colour the animal correctly.
- Repeat with the other rows.

  Answers: Row 1: a yellow cat, Row 2: a red hen, Row 3: a green rabbit

2 57 & 58 Listen and repeat. Trace and colour. Sing.

Introduce the number 5

- Hold up the flashcard with the number 5 and say *five*. Count your fingers, one by one and say *One, two, three, four, five!* Write the number 5 on the board several times, saying it each time.

 Now draw several sets of five items on the board, e.g. five flowers, five stars, five balls. Draw the same items close to each other. Ask Horsey to find five flowers. Make him count them and then draw a circle around them. Once Horsey has demonstrated the activity, ask children to come up to the board and circle five stars and five balls.

Introduce the number 6

- Hold up the flashcard with the number 6 and say *six*. Count five fingers on one hand and then hold up one more saying *One, two, three, four, five, six!* Write 6 on the board several times, saying the number each time.

 Now put five books or crayons on one side of the table and six books or crayons on the other. Give Horsey the flashcards with the numbers 5 and 6 and help him to count the items and put the flashcards in the correct place. Now let the children take turns to do the activity.

- See ideas for more number games on pages 22 and 32.

Use the book

- Point out that Bella has two new numbers. Point to 5 and encourage the children to say *five*. Count the cats together and say *one, two, three, four, five*. Count on your fingers and say the numbers. Help the children to do the same.

- Then do the same with the number 6. Count the birds and say *one, two, three, four, five, six*.

Play the CD

- Play the recording and encourage the children to repeat.

TRACK 57

Five [pause] *five* [pause] *five* [pause]
Six [pause] *six* [pause] *six* [pause]

- Help the children to trace the numbers 5 and 6 and colour the cats and the birds.

Play the song

- Play the CD and encourage the children to join in.

- Play the song again and let the children jump and skip as they sing.

TRACK 58

1 2 3 4 5 6
Jump, jump, jump, skip, skip, skip
1 2 3 4 5 6
Jump, jump, jump, skip, skip, skip!

Lesson aims

- To listen to a story which reviews the language of the unit.

- To act out the story.

- To become aware of the importance of being kind to animals.

Materials: hen, bird, cat or rabbit shapes, saucers of paint, small pieces of sponge (for each child); animal masks (see Lesson 7) (optional)

Warm up

- Craft Make sponge paintings. Draw hen, bird, cat or rabbit shapes for the children. Give them saucers of paint and small pieces of sponge. They dip the sponge in the paint and dab the shapes with the colour to make textured paintings. When the paint has dried, help them to add eyes, whiskers, noses or beaks.

1 🔊 59 Listen. Act it out.

- Help the children open their books at page 36.
- Give them time to look at the pictures and to say who they can see.
- Point to the pictures and see if the children can remember the names of the animals.
- Explain that in this story Horsey is followed by increasing amounts of animals and he ends up giving them all a ride. Say that he is kind to animals. Ask the children if they are kind to animals and if they say *Yes!* praise them.

Play the CD

- Play the recording several times while the children just listen.

TRACK 59

Jack: *Look at the rabbits, Horsey!*
Horsey: *Yes! Rabbits!*

Lily: *Look at the hens, Horsey!*
Horsey: *Yes! Rabbits and hens!*

Jack: *Look at the birds, Horsey!*
Horsey: *Rabbits and hens and birds!*

Lily: *Look at the cats, Horsey!*
Horsey: *Yes! Rabbits and hens and birds and cats!*

🎭 Act it out.

- 🐴 Play with Horsey puppet. Give one child the puppet and divide the rest of the class into rabbits, hens, birds and cats. You could give them flashcards or make animal masks (see Lesson 7). Help the class to chant the names of the animals, adding one more each time.
- Get the child who is playing Horsey to walk around the class. Then call out *Rabbits!* and the children who are rabbits follow Horsey. Then call out *Hens!* and the hens follow Horsey. Then call out *Birds!* and the birds join in. Finally, call out *Cats!* and the cats join in the parade.

Unit 5 Lesson 5

Lesson aims

- To review amounts up to three in a matching activity.

- To learn the sound of the letters *o* and *p* and associate them with *orange* and *pizza*.

Materials: a teddy, a circle of card, playdough, small decorations for pretend cakes, small candles or sticks, paper cupcake holders (optional); two different coloured balls of wool, four toy cars, six toy dolls; plasticine; a real orange, a plate; a photo of a pizza, an apron for each child, slices of bread (one for each child), round biscuit cutters, grated cheese, slices of tomato, a flat baking tray

Warm up

- Hold up a teddy. Tell the children that it is Teddy's birthday today and he is five years old (you can choose any age from *1–6*). Make Teddy a birthday badge from a circle of card and write the number *5* on it.
- Then ask the children if they would like to make cakes for Teddy. Give them playdough and small decorations to make pretend cakes. Give each table of children enough small candles or sticks so that they can each put five on their cakes. You could also give them paper cupcake holders to put their cakes in.

1 Match.

Introduce the activity

- Do matching activities with lengths of wool. Clear a space in the classroom and put two toy cars on one side and two more toy cars on the other side. Then put three dolls on one side and three more dolls on the other side.

- Give the children two different coloured balls of wool. Ask them to match the amounts with the wool, e.g. one child holds the wool next to the two cars and another child holds it at the other end next to the other two cars. Two more children do the same for the dolls.
- Repeat with different children.

Use the book

- Help the children open their books at page 37.
- This matching activity reviews counting up to three. As they point to the animals, encourage them to count out loud *One cat. One, two hens, One, two, three rabbits.*
- Help them trace over the sample line; then ask them to draw lines to match the other animals. They should draw lines from the two hens to the other two hens and from the three rabbits to the other three rabbits.

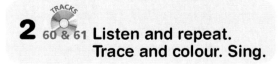

2 60 & 61 **Listen and repeat. Trace and colour. Sing.**

Introduce the letter *o*

- Show the flashcard of the letter *o* and say the sound. Write it on the board several times, saying the sound each time. Ask the children to tell you what shape the letter is and see if they can remember the word *circle*.
- Make Horsey excited about writing circular *o* shapes and then let the children take turns to come up to the front and write *o* on the board.
- Give the children plasticine and let them roll it into strips and make the letter *o*.

- Show the flashcard of an orange and say *orange*. Take a real orange into the class, hold it up and say *Orange. I've got an orange. Who likes oranges?* Make Horsey say *I like oranges!* Wash your hands and peel the orange and let a child hand around the pieces on a plate. Add more pieces and review numbers by telling the children they can have two or three pieces.

Introduce the letter *p*

- Show the flashcard of the letter *p* and say the sound. Write it on the board several times, saying the sound each time. Let the children come and trace over the letters with a different coloured marker or chalk.
- Show the flashcard of a pizza and say *pizza*. Make mini bread pizzas with the children. Show the children a photo of a pizza and tell them they are going to make some. All wash your hands and put on aprons. Give each child a slice of bread and a round biscuit cutter. Help them press out circular shapes from the bread. Give them grated cheese and slices of tomato and let them cover their bread circles with the toppings; their pizzas will be nicer if they put the tomato on first followed by the cheese. Let them all lay their bread pizzas on a flat baking tray and, if you have access to the school kitchens, take them to be grilled. Make sure the children know that they must always ask for help with the grilling. These mini bread pizzas can be eaten uncooked if you cannot grill them.
- See pages 20 and 45 for more letter games.

Tip If you do not have circular biscuit cutters, the children can cut the slices of bread into square shapes or triangles using round-edged knives. The cutting process will help their fine motor skills.

Use the book

- Show the children that Horsey has two new letters on his necklace. Point and say the sound for the letter *o*. Point to the orange and say /ɒ/, /ɒ/, /ɒ/, *orange*. Then point to the *p* and say the sound for the letter *p*. Point to the pizza and say /p/, /p/, /p/, *pizza*.

Play the CD

- Play the recording and encourage the children to repeat.

60

o orange
o o o o
orange

p pizza
p p p p
pizza

- Help the children to trace the letters *o* and *p* and to colour the orange and the pizza.

Play the song

- Remind the children of the *Alphabet* song they have learnt so far and sing it together.
- Tell them that they are going to learn two more names of letters today. Hold up the flashcards of the letters *o* and *p* and say the names, *o* and *p*. Repeat a few times and encourage the children to say the names.

- Play the CD and encourage the children to join in with the song.
- See page 25 for Teacher's notes on playing the *Eat the letter* game.

TRACK 61

a b c
d e f
g h i
j k l
m n o p

Unit 5 Lesson 6

Lesson aim

- To learn about animals which are awake at night.

Materials: a shoebox, small blankets or sheets for each child (optional); a picture of daytime and a picture of night; sun and moon shapes cut from card, craft sticks for each child; pictures of an owl, a bat, a fox, the sun and the moon

Warm up

-   Play the *Goodnight* game. Make a little bed for Horsey in a shoebox. Tell the children that Horsey is tired and wants to go to bed. Say *Goodnight, Horsey!* Give him a kiss and put him to bed. Then encourage the children to be very quiet because Horsey is asleep. After a while, make Horsey wake up. Say *Good morning, Horsey!*
- Once you have demonstrated the game with Horsey, play it with the children. Say *Goodnight!* and let them lay their heads on their tables and pretend to be asleep (or lie on the floor). You could give them small blankets or sheets as they pretend to sleep. Then say *Good morning!* and they mime waking up.

1 Match.

Introduce the topic

- Find two pictures, one showing daytime and one showing night and attach them to the board (or you could draw a sun and a moon on the board). Ask the children when they come to school and help them to point to the correct picture. Do the same for other activities, when they go to bed, dream, have a bath or shower, eat lunch, play with their friends. Ask them if they do most things in the day or the night.
- Now tell them that they are going to learn about three animals that are awake when we are asleep.

Use the book

- Help the children open their books at page 38.
- Look at the photos along the top and see if the children know what these creatures are. Point to each one and say their names clearly *owl, bat, fox*.
- Explain to the children that these animals sleep during the day and wake up at night.
- Point to the sample matching line and let the children work out which animal photos match the other animal silhouettes in the main picture. Then help them to draw matching lines between these.

 Make suns and moons.

- Give the children sun and moon shapes cut from card. Let them paint them or colour them with crayons. Paste these onto craft sticks.

 Night and day.

- Play the *Goodnight* game again and let the children pretend to go to sleep at their desks. Now give three children pictures of an owl, a bat and a fox and let them run around while the children are 'sleeping'.
- You could also give two children a picture of the sun and the moon (or use the sun and moon shapes from the craft activity). The one with the sun holds up their picture and the owl, bat and fox go to sleep and the children wake up. Then the other child holds up the moon and the owl, bat and fox wake up and the children go to sleep.

Unit 5 Lesson 7

Lesson aims

- To match animal masks to photos of the animals.
- To make animals masks.
- To learn the colour *blue* and become aware of the shape *rectangle*.

Materials: red, green and yellow items, e.g. toy cars and bricks, a large box; a picture of an owl; paper plates (one for each child), triangles of card, pipe cleaners or strips of stiff card, feathery strips of paper, sponges, black, white, grey, orange, brown paint, large card rabbit ears, strips of card or pipe cleaners, craft sticks (see teacher's website); blue items, e.g. toy cars, two paper bags; pots of light blue and dark blue paint, big paintbrushes, sun and moon stickers or shapes, cotton wool for each child; circular and rectangular items, e.g. paper, books, coins, buttons, paper plates

Warm up

- Review the colours learnt so far (red, green and yellow). Gather together items which are either red, green or yellow, e.g. pencils, crayons, toy cars, bricks, etc. Help the children arrange them into three different groups in the classroom – all the red items in one place, all the green items in another and all the yellow ones in another.

- Place a large box in the middle of the class. Now call out a colour and let the children go and choose one item of that colour and place it in the box. You could make this more challenging by calling out the name of the item too, e.g. *red crayon* or *yellow car*. When the children feel comfortable with this, add amounts too, e.g. *Two red crayons! Three green cars!* Help them to gather the correct amounts.

- Now make the game more fun by telling the children to hop, skip or jump as they get the items and put them in the box.

> **Tip** As you gradually increase the children's comprehension in this way, do not worry if they do not all understand or if some are just copying the others. Backtrack and give the children a simpler command so that they can all join in.

1 Match.

Introduce the activity

- Take flashcards of a cat and a rabbit and a picture of an owl. Put them on the board and let the children call out the names as you and Horsey point to them.

- Now start to draw the top of the head of the owl on the board. Draw the pointed ear tufts and the big eyes and ask the children *What's this? Is it a rabbit? Is it a cat?* Help them to answer *No! Owl!* Do this question and answer activity with Horsey first so that the children know what to say. Then draw the long ears of a rabbit and ask again and finally the eyes and ears of a cat.

- You could draw other parts of these creatures too, e.g. their noses or beaks, their markings or feathers.

- Demonstrate the Cat and Rabbit yoga poses (see teacher's website) and encourage the children to join in.

> **Tip** Children are innately interested in nature. They will probably be interested to know that owls' ears are at the side of their head and, unlike our ears, they are not level. Owls have very good hearing and their uneven ears help them to hear different sounds coming from different directions.

Use the book

- Help the children open their books at page 39.
- Point to the photos of the animals and encourage the children to call out their names (owl, rabbit and cat).

- Now point to the masks and show the sample line. Let the children work out which masks match which photos and help them to draw matching lines.

 Make animal masks.

- Take paper plates and cut out the centres so that the children have face holes in their masks. Let them decide which animal mask they would like to make (see teacher's website, http://www.macmillanyoung learners.com/learningstars/teacher):

For cats: give the children triangles of card for ears and pipe cleaners or strips of stiff card to make whiskers. They could paint their masks black, white, grey or orange.

For owls: give the children feathery strips of paper to make ear tufts. They could sponge paint the plates with grey, white and brown paint to make textured, feathery faces.

For rabbits: give the children large card ears and strips of card or pipe cleaners for whiskers. They could paint their plates white, grey, brown or black.

- When the plates have dried, attach craft sticks to them. Let the children have fun holding them up in front of their faces so they can see through and pretending to make animal sounds and movements.

 **2** 62 & 63 **Listen and repeat. Colour. Sing.**

Introduce the colour *blue*

- Show the flashcard of the colour blue and say *blue*. Gather together blue items, e.g. cars, crayons and paints. Point and say *Blue, a blue car. Blue, a blue crayon.*

 Ask the children to find something blue in the classroom and come up to the front and give it to Horsey. You could give Horsey two paper bags – one with the colour blue on it and one with another of the colours they have learnt so far. Make Horsey say *Thank you!* when he receives his coloured items.

 Make night sky, day sky pictures.

- Give the children white sheets of paper, pots of light blue paint and big paintbrushes. Let them have fun making big strokes across the paper until they have covered it.

- Then give them dark blue paint and let them do the same on different sheets of paper. Ask them which sky we see in the day and which one at night.

- Give them sun and moon stickers or shapes to stick on the appropriate pictures. They can make white clouds by pulling apart cotton wool and glueing it in place.

Introduce the shape *rectangle*

- Show the flashcard of the rectangle shape and say *rectangle*. Draw a rectangle on the board and say *Rectangle. It's a rectangle.* Then draw a circle and say *Circle. It's a circle.* On a table place items which are circular and items which are rectangular, e.g. pieces of paper, books, coins, buttons, paper plates. Have the children sort them into piles of the same shape.

Use the book

- Point to the blue rectangle. Say *blue*. Draw a rectangle on the board and say *rectangle*.

- Ask them to open their books at page 3 and see if they can find the same shape on the rug.

- Point to the picture of the sky and say *Sky. The sky is blue.* Look outside the window and ask them if the sky is blue today.

Play the CD

- Play the recording and encourage the children to repeat.

 TRACK 62

Blue, blue, blue
Sky! Sky!

- Show the flashcard of the sky and say *sky*. Help the children to colour the sky in their books blue. Ask the children to name other natural things which are blue, e.g. sea.

- Have the children look and point to things that are rectangles in the classroom.

Play the song

- Play the CD and encourage the children to join in.

- Sing the song again and point upwards as you sing *sky*.

TRACK 63

Blue, blue, blue,
Blue, blue, blue,
Sky! Sky!
Blue, blue, blue.

Unit 6 Food

By the end of Unit 6 the children will be able to:

- say the food and drink words: *juice, sandwich, grapes, apple, water, cake.*
- perform the routine of washing and drying their hands.
- say the sounds, sing the names and trace the letters *q, r, s, t.*
- recognise that *queen* goes with *q*, *rabbit* with *r*, *sun* with *s* and *tomato* with *t*.
- recognise and say the numbers *7* and *8* and understand the amounts.
- understand how bread is made and recognise different forms of bread.
- recognise and say the colour *white* and be aware of a cloud shape.
- help make an apple tree print picture.

New/Reviewed words and language

juice, sandwich, grapes, apple, water, cake
I like (sandwiches).
/kw/, /r/, /s/, /t/, *q, r, s, t*
queen, rabbit, sun, tomato
7, seven, 8, eight
bread
white, cloud

Classroom language

Here you are. Thank you!
What has (Lily) got? She's got a (sandwich).
Wash your hands. Dry your hands.
Colour the (cakes).

Value of the unit

I wash my hands.

Materials

scissors, glue, crayons, pencils, paper, card, paints
Horsey puppet
flashcards
CD

Lesson aims

- To learn/review and say the words: *juice, sandwich, grapes, apple, water, cake.*
- To learn the sound of the letter *q* and associate it with *queen.*

Materials: a paper plate, an apple (optional); real or toy food (e.g. sandwiches, grapes, apples, cake), some water, some juice (or pictures of these items), tablecloths, paper plates and cups for each table; pictures from magazines of the food items (see teacher's website), paper plates for each child; large pieces of card, pictures of food from the unit, a picture of a restaurant (optional); crown template (one for each child) (see teacher's website), coloured foil shapes, stickers, glitter, sticky tape; lengths of material, old tablecloths or curtains (optional)

Warm up

- 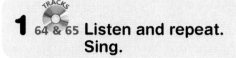 Play a game which encourages courtesy and good table manners. Have everyone sit in a circle. Hold a paper plate and hand it to Horsey. Say *Here you are.* Make Horsey say *Thank you!* Now make Horsey hand the plate to another child and say *Here you are.* Encourage the child to say *Thank you!* and pass it on. Go around the circle in this way.

- You could make this more challenging by balancing an apple on the plate as you pass it around.

1 64 & 65 Listen and repeat. Sing.

Introduce the vocabulary

- Use the food and drink flashcards. Hold up each one and say the words clearly. Repeat and encourage the children to say the words with you.

- If you can, have actual food and drink for this activity, e.g. sandwiches, grapes, apples, cake, some water and some juice. If this is not possible, use plastic toy food or pictures.

- Ask everyone to wash their hands. With the children, lay tablecloths on the children's tables and let the children help to lay the table with paper plates and cups. You can review counting and amounts while you do this. Count the children around one table (*one, two, three, four, five, six*). Then count out the paper plates and cups in the same way. Now put the food on the plates and pour water or juice into cups. Say the names of each as you do so.

 Make plates of food.

- Find pictures from magazines or draw the food items you are teaching (e.g. grapes, apples, sandwiches, cake). Cut them out and let the children glue them to paper plates. You can find plates with images of food stuck on them on the teacher's website, http://www.macmillanyounglearners.com/learningstars/teacher.

Use the book

- Help the children open their books at page 40.

- Let the children point to Horsey, Bella, Jack and Lily and say their names.

- Point to the food on the table and say the words clearly, *sandwich, grapes, apple, juice, water, cake.*

Play the CD

- Play the recording and encourage the children to repeat.

 juice
sandwich
grapes
apple
water
cake

- Play the CD again and encourage the children to point to the pictures as they say the words.

- Ask them *What has Jack got?* (cake and water). *What has Lily got?* (a sandwich and juice). *What has Horsey got?* (an apple). *What has Bella got?* (grapes).

- Now draw attention to the menu. Encourage the children to point and say the items. Give the children time to match the pictures on the menu to the food on the table.

- Ask if the children can see any triangles in the picture. The sandwiches are triangles. Count them: *one, two.* Then ask what colour the apple is.

- Finally, ask the children which of the food items they like. Point to the grapes and say *I like grapes.* Rub your tummy and look happy as you say this.

Play the song

- Play the CD and encourage the children to join in.

- Sing the song again and hold up play food items or flashcards as you do so.

 I like sandwiches, I like grapes
I like apples, I like cake
I like water and I like juice
Yes, yes, I do
Yes, I do, yes, I do
Yes, I do, yes, I do
Yes, I do, yes, I do
I like sandwiches, I like grapes
I like apples, I like cake
I like water and I like juice
Yes, yes, I do!

Make picture menus.

- Give the children large pieces of card and help them to fold them in half.

- Glue pictures of the food from the unit onto the card. The children can pretend that these are menus and order from them. Help them to say *A sandwich, please.*

- You could extend this activity by thinking of a name for your 'class restaurant' and decorating the front of the menu with that title and a picture of a restaurant.

 2 **Listen and repeat. Trace and colour.**

Introduce the letter *q*

- Show the flashcard of the letter *q* and say the sound. Write it on the board several times, saying the sound each time. Then write some of the other letters from *a–p* on the board. Say the /kw/ sound and ask Horsey to find the correct letter. Then let the children find them and circle them with markers or chalk.

- See pages 20 and 45 for more letter games.

 Make crowns.

- Make simple paper crowns with the children. Give each one a crown template (see template on the teacher's website, http://www.macmillanyounglearners.com/learningstars/teacher). Let them decide if they want to be kings or queens. Give the children coloured foil shapes, stickers and glitter and let them colour and decorate their crowns. Put the crowns around each child's head and attach the ends with sticky tape.

 Pretend to be kings and queens.

- Tell the children that kings and queens walk in a majestic way. Have fun walking around the classroom in a stately fashion with your heads held high. You could improvise cloaks and capes from lengths of material, old tablecloths or curtains. Practise bowing and curtsying. Play around with language as you do this. For example, bow very low and say *Good morning, your majesty!* Kings and queens might speak in a different manner too – let the children say *Hello!* to you in funny voices, pretending to be regal.

Use the book

- Point to Horsey and say that he has the letter *q* on his necklace today. Let the children say the sound /kw/. Point to the queen and say *queen*. Say /kw/, /kw/, /kw/, *queen*. Show the flashcard of a queen and say *queen*.

Play the CD

- Play the recording and encourage the children to repeat.

TRACK 66

q queen
q q q q
queen

- Help the children to trace the letter *q* and colour the queen.

Unit 6 Lesson 2

Lesson aims

- To become familiar with the classroom routine of washing and drying hands.

- To learn the sound of the letter *r* and associate it with *rabbit*.

Materials: a small towel (one for each child); a bar of soap (one for each child), jugs and bowls of water (optional); a picture of a rabbit

Warm up

- Practise folding up towels together. Give each child a small towel and show them how to fold it in half and then half again. When they have all folded their towels, help them to put them into neat piles. Then let one child at a time carry a pile and put it in a drawer or on a shelf.

1 🔘 TRACK 67 Match. Sing.

Introduce the routine

- Ideally, you should introduce this activity in the school bathrooms. Make sure you have enough bars of soap and clean towels for everyone. Show the children how to wash their hands properly, rinse them and dry them.
- If you cannot all visit the school bathroom, have jugs and bowls of water in the classroom.

Use the book

- Help the children open their books at page 41.
- Point to the first picture of the girl washing her hands and say *Wash your hands.* Mime the action and encourage the children to copy you. Do the same with the second picture of the girl drying her hands and say *Dry your hands.*
- Let the children look at the pictures of the soap and towel below and see if they can work out which girl they should go with. Help them to draw matching lines. Note that from Unit 6 onwards not all of the matching activities have a sample line. The children should be familiar with this activity type by now.

Play the song

- Play the CD and encourage the children to join in.
- Play the song again and the children mime the actions as they sing.

- You can sing this song as part of a classroom routine each time the children really wash and dry their hands.

🔘 TRACK 67
Wash your hands, wash your hands,
Splash, splash, wash your hands.
Wash your hands, wash your hands,
Splash, splash, wash your hands.

Dry your hands, dry your hands,
Rub, rub, dry your hands.
Dry your hands, dry your hands,
Rub, rub, dry your hands.

2 🔘 TRACK 68 Listen and repeat. Trace and colour.

Introduce the letter *r*

- Show the flashcard of the letter *r* and say the sound. Write it on the board several times, saying the sound each time. Write other letters from *a–q* around them and then let Horsey and the children identify and circle the letter sounds you call out.

- 🔘 TRACK 53 Show a picture or the flashcard of a rabbit. See if the children can remember the word. Sing the *Animals* song from Unit 5, Lesson 1 and encourage the children to hop like rabbits.
- See pages 20 and 45 for more letter games.

Use the book

- Show the children that Horsey has the letter *r* on his necklace today. Say the sound again. Say /r/, /r/, /r/, *rabbit.*

Play the CD

- Play the recording and encourage the children to repeat.

🔘 TRACK 68
r rabbit
r r r r
rabbit

- Help the children to trace the letter *r* and colour the rabbit.

Unit 6 Lesson 3

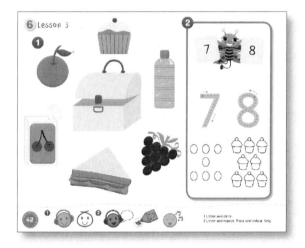

Lesson aims

- To recognise food words in a simple dialogue.
- To learn the numbers *7* and *8* and become aware of the amounts.

Materials: music, a drum, a triangle (optional); ten items (e.g. cars, bricks), a bag (optional); sand trays; paper plates (one for each child), bunches of grapes, pictures of cakes for each child (optional), playdough; a packet of small plain cakes (one cake for each child), an apron for each child, a big bowl, soft butter, icing sugar, vanilla essence (optional), a little milk (optional), a wooden spoon, a teaspoon for each child, a flat knife for each child, edible cake decorations

Warm up

- 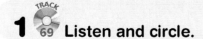 Play a walking game. Put some music on and lead the children around the classroom making very big steps. Say *Big step, big step* each time. Then change and take very small steps. Say *Small step, small step* as you do so.

- You could bang a drum in time with the big steps and a triangle in time with the small steps to make the difference more obvious.

1 TRACK 69 Listen and circle.

Introduce the activity

- Ask the children to open their own lunchboxes and show everyone what they have got to eat today. Look at them one by one and name the items the children already know, e.g. *sandwich, water, juice, grapes, apple, cake.* Say *Look, (Helen)'s got water. Oh, (Sam)'s got juice.*

- Then play a guessing game, using the same lunchboxes. Say *She's got a sandwich and water.* Help the children to guess which child you are talking about.

Tip In the game described in the left-hand column you will be using the third person singular form *has got*. In the listening activity, the children will hear the first person singular *have got*. The children will understand and you do not have to give any explanations; for them the nouns are the recognisable part of the sentence.

Use the book

- Help the children open their books at page 42.

- Let them point to the pictures of food and drinks and say what they can see.

- Now tell them they are going to listen to a child talking about what is in his lunchbox. When they hear a food or drink word, they should find and point to the correct picture.

Play the CD

- Play the recording through once and check that the children are pointing to the correct pictures.

- Then play it again and pause after the child mentions each item of food or drink. Help them to find the correct picture and then to circle it.

Answers: sandwich, water, grapes

TRACK 69

Boy: *I've got a sandwich.*
Teacher: *A sandwich?*
Boy: *Yes, a sandwich! And … water.*
Teacher: *Water?*
Boy: *Yes, water. And … grapes.*
Teacher: *Oh, grapes!*
Boy: *Yes! Grapes!*

---

2 TRACKS 70 & 71 Listen and repeat. Trace and colour. Sing.

Introduce the number 7

- Show the flashcard of the number *7* and say *seven.* Hold up seven fingers, counting them as you do so. Write the number *7* on the board several times. Let the children come and trace over the numbers.

- Now put ten items on a table, e.g. crayons, cars, bricks, books. Ask Horsey to count out seven of them. Make Horsey forget the numbers halfway through *One, two, three, four … mmm.* Encourage the children to join in and help him.

- Then let children take turns to come up to the front and count seven items and give them to you. You could give them a bag to put them in, as they might not be able to hold that many items.

Introduce the number 8

- Hold up the flashcard with the number *8* and say the word. Write it on the board. Show the children how you are doing one big swirling, curving line to write it, not putting two circles one on top of the other. Let them have fun trying to draw those big swirling lines. It does not matter if their number 8s turn out wrong, they will enjoy writing in this way.

- Give them sand trays to write the numbers *7* and *8* in.

- Now put ten items on the table and ask children to take turns to bring you eight of them.

- See ideas for more number games on pages 22 and 32.

Play *Do a long jump.*

- In the playground draw eight squares in a long line. Write the numbers *1–8* in them and encourage the children to count *1–8* as you do so.

- Now draw a starting line, from where they should begin to jump. Let each child have a turn to see how far they can jump. Can they reach number 3? Can they jump further?

Use the book

- Show the children that Bella has two numbers today and ask them to point and say *seven* then *eight*. Point to the grapes and the cakes and count them together.

Play the CD

- Play the recording and encourage the children to repeat.

Seven [pause] *seven* [pause] *seven* [pause]
Eight [pause] *eight* [pause] *eight* [pause]

- Help the children to trace the numbers *7* and *8* and colour the pictures.

Play the song

- Play the CD and encourage the children to join in.

1 2 3 4 5 6 7
Seven grapes on my plate.
1 2 3 4 5 6 7 8
Eight cakes on my plate.

- Give the children paper plates and bunches of grapes. Let them count out eight grapes to put on their plates. You could give them little pictures of cakes to put on plates too, or get them to make some small cake shapes out of playdough.

Cookery activity: decorating cupcakes

- Bring in a packet of small plain cakes. All wash your hands and put on aprons.

- Make a big bowl of icing with soft butter and icing sugar. You can add a little vanilla essence and a drop of milk to make it softer. Mix it with a wooden spoon.

- Then give the children teaspoons and let them spoon some icing onto their cakes. Give them flat knives and show them how to spread it all over the top. They can use the back of the spoon for this too.

- Then give them edible cake decorations to sprinkle on top.

> **Tip** Always encourage healthy eating at school. Ask parents to pack healthy food like salads, brown bread sandwiches, water, juice and fruit in their lunchboxes. However, you could let the children have treats once a week.

Lesson aims

- To listen to a story which reviews the language of the unit.

- To act out the story.

Materials: cutlery, plates, plastic drinking cups, toys; a box, wrapping paper, a big teddy, play food or pictures of food glued onto card, real fruit and vegetables (optional), old food cartons (optional), a potato (optional)

Warm up

- Put a variety of items on a table, including cutlery, plates and plastic drinking cups. Add other general items, e.g. toys, pencils, paper and so on. Ask the children to find and sort the items we need when we have dinner with our family at home. Ask them if we want toy cars on the table or if we should put them in the toy box.

1 Listen. Act it out.

Introduce the activity

- Decorate a box with wrapping paper. Take a big teddy and sit him next to the box. Tell the children that the box is Teddy's lunchbox. Ask them to suggest what they think he might like in his lunchbox. Provide play food or pictures of food glued onto card and get the children to put the food items into the lunchbox. You could use real fruit and vegetables and old cartons of food too.

- Have fun with this and do not feel that you have to stick rigidly to the food items the children have learnt. For example, you could hold up a picture of some potatoes and ask Teddy *Do you like potatoes, Teddy?* Make him nod enthusiastically and say *Yes!* Let the children put the potatoes in the box. You could make Horsey watch this with interest and thus set the scene for the story.

Use the book

- Help the children open their books at page 43.

- Let the children look at the pictures and point and say what they can see. Ask questions in L1, e.g. What have Jack and Lily got in their lunchboxes? What about Horsey? Do they think he has got too much?

Play the CD

- Play the recording several times while the children just listen.

Jack: *I like sandwiches.*
Horsey: *I like sandwiches!*

Lily: *I like grapes.*
Horsey: *I like grapes!*
Jack: *I like apples.*
Horsey: *I like apples!*

Lily: *I like water.*
Horsey: *I like water!*
Jack: *I like juice.*

Jack and Lily: *Horsey!*

Act it out.

- Let the children pretend to be Jack, Lily and Horsey packing their lunchboxes. They might remember the words the characters said in the story, but they might like to improvise too. You could use the same box and the food items that you used at the beginning of Activity 1 in the left-hand column.

- Play with them and when they say *I like apples*, say *I like apples!* Say it again and again then swap roles and say *I like water* so that they can say *I like water!*

Unit 6 Lesson 5

Lesson aims

- To review the food words: *cake, juice, apple* and *sandwich*.

- To review shapes: *triangle, rectangle, circle* and *square*.

- To develop cognitive skills by matching flat shapes to 3D items.

- To learn the sounds of the letters *s* and *t* and associate them with *sun* and *tomato*.

Materials: lengths of wool, circle, square, triangle and rectangle shapes; card cut into different shapes and of different colours; a real tomato or a play food tomato

Warm up

- Draw the four shapes on the board one at a time. Say the words and encourage the children to repeat. Then point to each one and the children say the word. Do this in random order and more and more quickly.

1 Match.

Introduce the activity

- Make shapes with wool. Give each child several lengths of wool. Hold up a circle shape and ask them to make a circle with their wool. Horsey can help them to do this. Then do the same with squares, triangles and rectangles. Encourage them to say the name of the shapes as they play.

Use the book

- Help the children open their books at page 44.
- Let them point and say the food and drink words (cake, juice, apple and sandwich).
- Give them time to see if they can match the foods to the shapes on the tablecloth. Help them with this and to draw matching lines between each one.

  Answers: cake – triangle, juice – rectangle, apple – circle, sandwich – square

Craft Make card food.

- Make card food with different shapes. Give the children several colours and shapes and let them decide which foods they look like. Help them to add markings to make tomatoes, apples, sandwiches, grapes and so on.

---

2 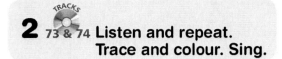 73 & 74 Listen and repeat. Trace and colour. Sing.

Introduce the letter *s*

- Show the flashcard of the letter *s* and say the sound. Write it several times on the board, saying the sound each time. Show the children that it is a nice, wriggly letter and let them have fun trying to draw it. Do not focus on accuracy at this point.
- Hold up the flashcard of the sun. See if they remember it from Unit 5, Lesson 6. Ask if we see the sun in the day or the night. Then ask if they remember whether bats and owls like the sun or the moon better.
- Stand like suns with your arms and legs outstretched like rays. Ask questions in L1, e.g. What colour is the sun and what shape is it? Is it always yellow? What about when it sets at night, what colour is it then? Remind the children that we must never look directly at the sun because it will hurt our eyes.

Introduce the letter *t*

- Show the flashcard of the letter *t* and say the sound. Write it several times on the board, saying the sound each time. Show them that *t* is a nice easy letter to write – a straight line down with a curve and a little line going across it near the top. Say *long line, short line* as you write it. Let them play at tracing it and trying to write it on the board. Again, do not focus on accuracy at this point but on them becoming dexterous with pens, markers and chalk.

- 24 Show the flashcard of the tomato and/ or a real tomato or a play food tomato. Prompt them to say *tomato*. Ask what colour it is and prompt them to say *red*. Play the *Red tomato* song and encourage the children to join in.
- See pages 20 and 45 for more letter games.

Use the book

- Show the children that Horsey has two new letters on his necklace and help them to point and say the sounds. Then say *Sun.* /s/, /s/, /s/, *sun. Tomato.* /t/, /t/, /t/, *tomato*.

Play the CD

- Play the recording and encourage the children to repeat.

---

73   *s sun*
       s s s s
       sun

       t tomato
       t t t t
       tomato

- Help the children to trace the letters *s* and *t* and colour the pictures.

Play the song

- Now see if they can sing the *Alphabet* song they have learnt so far. Tell them they will sing four new names of letters today, *q, r, s* and *t*.
- Play the CD and encourage the children to join in.
- Put flashcards of the letters on the board. Play the song several times and let the children join in and point to the letters as they do so.

- See page 25 for Teacher's notes on playing the *Eat the letter* game.

See page 25 for Teacher's notes on playing the *Eat the letter* game.

TRACK 74

a b c
d e f
g h i
j k l
m n o p
q r s t

Unit 6 Lesson 6

6 Lesson 6   Big Wide World

Lesson aim

- To become aware of how bread is made and recognise bread in different forms.

Materials: ingredients to make a simple tomato sandwich (optional); bread dough (optional) (see list of ingredients and materials needed in recipe opposite), an apron for each child

Warm up

- If possible, bring in a simple tomato sandwich (or draw one on the board). Say *sandwich*. Open it up and point and say *tomato*. Hold up the slice of bread and say *bread*. Put it back together again and say *I like sandwiches! Yum, yum!*

1 Colour.

Introduce the topic

- If it is possible, make bread dough in the class with the children. All wash your hands and put on aprons. There are lots of different bread recipes, but you could try the one opposite.

Use the book

- Help the children open their books at page 45.
- Let them look at the photos of bread being made and ask which of these things they did when you made bread together. Ask them to point to which of these they liked best.
- Now look at the pictures of food below and ask them to find the ones which show *bread*. Let the children point and say *bread* and then colour the stars next to those pictures only (i.e. the slice of bread, the roll and the loaf).

> **Tip** The activity asks for the children to colour the stars next to the pictures of bread only. Some children might colour all the stars. This does not necessarily mean they have not understood; they might just like colouring stars. Check comprehension by asking them to point to the bread pictures.

Bread recipe

Ingredients:

- 500 grams of wheat flour
- 1 sachet of yeast
- 2 tablespoons of olive oil
- I teaspoon of salt
- I tablespoon of honey
- 300 ml of hot (not boiling) water

Method:

Put the flour, yeast and salt in a big bowl and mix it all up with your hands.

In a separate jug mix up the hot water, the oil and the honey with a spoon.

Add the liquid ingredients to the dry ones. Mix it all up with your hands.

Cover a clean table with some flour. Tip the dough onto this floured surface and knead it, pushing and pulling it to make it nice and soft.

Oil a bread tin and put the kneaded dough into it. Put the tin with the dough into a plastic bag. Now leave it for an hour to rise.

Take the bread to the school kitchen and ask for it to be put in an oven which has been heated to 200C. Before you put it in the oven, make some slashes with a knife across the top of the dough.

Bake the bread for about 30–35 minutes.

Enjoy eating your delicious bread together!

> **Tip** The word *dough* is pronounced to rhyme with *so*. The word *knead* is pronounced like the word *need*.

Unit 6 Lesson 7

Lesson aims

- To make an apple tree print picture.
- To match fruits to trees.
- To learn the colour *white* and become aware of a cloud shape.

Materials: fruit, pictures of fruit trees; apples, a painting apron for each child, a large piece of paper for each table, pots of brown paint, pots of green paint, pots of water, large paintbrushes, cloths, a knife, craft sticks or lollipop sticks, saucers of red paint, saucers of green paint (see teacher's website); sheets of blue paper (one for each child), glue sticks, white cotton wool

Warm up

- Demonstrate the Tree and Cloud yoga poses (see teacher's website) and encourage the children to join in.

 Grow like a tree.

- Curl up very small and gradually unfurl and 'grow' like a tree. Spread your arms and then your hands and finally wiggle your fingers. Shake one leg and then the other, stand strong on your feet and wiggle your toes. You can sway in the wind and make noises as if the breeze is rustling your leaves. Encourage the children to copy you and join in. Repeat a few times.

1 Make.

Introduce the activity

- Bring some fruit into the classroom and ask the children if they know where they grow. Do they grow in the ground or on trees? Find some pictures of fruit trees to show them. Ask if anyone has a fruit tree in their garden.
- Ask them if they think all the trees look the same. What about their leaves – how are they different? Help the children to notice differences. Tell them that today they are going to make big pictures of apple trees (see teacher's website, http://www.macmillanyounglearners.com/learning stars/teacher).

Use the book

- Help the children open their books at page 46.
- Draw their attention to the picture of the tree at the top.
- Have a supply of apples in the classroom. Get the children to put on painting aprons.

- On large pieces of paper, draw trunks and branches of trees with the children. Make one for each table as this is a group project. Give the children pots of brown paint, pots of green paint, pots of water, large paintbrushes and cloths to wipe their brushes. Let them paint the trees brown and add splodges of green for leaves.
- Slice the apples in half horizontally. Remove the seeds and push a craft stick or lollipop stick into the top of each apple half. Give the children saucers of red paint and of green paint. Show them how to dip the apples into the paint and make prints. Do this on spare paper first so that they can practise. Now let them print red and/or green apples onto their trees.
- Display the finished trees around the classroom.

2 Match. Colour.

- Let the children point to the pictures and say the words they know (tree, orange, lemon, apple). Ask them what colour the fruits are (orange, yellow and red).
- Give them time to match the fruits to the correct trees. Help them to trace over the sample line; then ask them to draw matching lines and then to colour the fruit. They might want to colour the apples green and that is fine.

3 75 & 76 **Listen and repeat. Colour. Sing.**

Introduce the colour *white*

- Show the flashcard with the colour white and say *white*. Ask the children to look around the class to find things which are white, for example, paper, pages in their books, crayons, light switches, the ceiling. Help them to think laterally by suggesting things which are not objects – their teeth, the whites of their eyes and so on.

Introduce the cloud shape

- Show the flashcard of the cloud shape and say *cloud*. Draw a cloud shape and say *Cloud. It's a cloud.* Look outside and ask if there are any clouds in the sky today. Then ask if clouds are always white. Sometimes they are grey and sometimes they are almost black. What about in the evening when the sun goes down, what colour are they then?

- Ask about their shapes: do clouds always stay the same shape? Children often find it easy to see different forms in cloud shapes; this can be nurtured. If there are clouds in the sky, all go out and watch them. Prompt them to tell you what they think the clouds look like.

 Make cotton wool clouds.

- Give the children sheets of blue paper, glue and white cotton wool. Let them have fun tearing apart the cotton wool and glueing it to the paper in cloud shapes.

Use the book

- Point to the cloud shape next to the tent. Say *white*. Draw a cloud with your finger. Say *Cloud. A white cloud.*

- Ask them to open their books at pages 2 and 3 and see if they can find the same cloud shape in Lessons 1 and 2.

- Point to the cloud below and say *cloud* again.

Play the CD

- Play the recording and encourage the children to repeat.

75
White, white, white
Cloud! Cloud!

- Give the children some white cotton wool and help them to glue this to the cloud. Ask the children to name other things which are white, e.g. snow, sugar, salt.

Play the song

- Play the CD and encourage the children to join in.

76
White, white, white,
White, white, white,
Cloud! Cloud!
White, white, white.

 Dance like clouds.

- Encourage the children to pretend to be clouds floating in the sky as you dance – change shapes, sway, wave your arms around. Maybe you are thunderclouds and could make big booming noises, or maybe you are little wispy clouds, whirling around the sky.

Lesson aim

- To review the main vocabulary of Units 5 and 6.

Materials: soft balls or beanbags, boxes

Warm up

- Play a throwing game. Give the children soft balls or beanbags. Put some open boxes at one end of the room. Put flashcards next to the boxes, e.g. alphabet cards, number cards or picture cards.

- Say the sound, number or word of the box you want the children to throw the ball into, e.g. *Two!* The children try to throw the ball into the correct box, e.g. with the number *2* flashcard next to it.

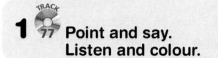

1 **Point and say.**
Listen and colour.

Introduce the activity

- Put flashcards of a sandwich, grapes, water, a cat, a bird and a rabbit on the board. Next to each one draw a small star outline. Say one of the words and let Horsey find the correct picture and colour the star by that picture. Continue with the other words and let the children come up to the board and colour the stars.

Use the book

- Help the children open their books at pages 47 and 48.

- Let the children point to the pictures and say the words.

Play the CD

- Play the recording and encourage the children to listen.

- Play the CD again. Pause after each word to give the children time to find the matching picture. They then colour the star next to it. Tell the children that if they cannot see the picture on the first page, they will have to turn the page over to look at the pictures on the second page.

---

sandwich
rabbit
grapes
water
cat
bird

Unit (7) Clothes

By the end of Unit 7 the children will be able to:

- say the clothes words: *shoes, socks, trousers, skirt, T-shirt.*
- perform the routine of taking their shoes off inside and putting them on to go out.
- say the sounds, sing the names and trace the letters *u, v* and *w.*
- recognise that *umbrella* goes with *u, van* with *v* and *window* with *w.*
- recognise and say the number *9* and understand the amount.
- recognise the difference between the emotions and say the words *happy* and *sad.*
- recognise and say the colour *black* and be aware of the shape *diamond.*
- make paper dolls.

New words and language

shoes, socks, trousers, skirt, T-shirt
Look at me!
/ʌ/, /v/, /w/, u, v, w
umbrella, van, window
9, nine
How are you today? I'm fine!
happy, sad
black, diamond

Classroom language

It's time to get dressed.
Give me the (T-shirt), please.
Take your shoes off, please.
Put your shoes on, please.
What colour are her (shoes)?
Colour the (bat).

Value of the unit

I take my shoes off in the house.

Materials

scissors, glue, paper, card, paints, a hole punch, crayons, pencils
Horsey puppet
flashcards
CD

Lesson aims

- To learn and say the clothes words: *shoes, socks, trousers, skirt, T-shirt.*
- To learn the sound of the letter *u* and associate it with *umbrella.*

Materials: a rug on the floor, a T-shirt for each child; doll's clothes or small children's clothes or baby clothes (shoes, socks, trousers, a skirt, a T-shirt), a teddy or a doll; a marker pen, uninflated balloons; a real umbrella (optional); a pack of coloured cupcake paper cases, pipe cleaners or card (optional), cotton wool (optional), blue glitter (see teacher's website)

82

Warm up

- Fold clothes together. Place a rug on the floor for the children to sit on while they do this. Give them T-shirts to fold. Show them how to make just one fold. If they can manage this easily, show them how to fold the sleeves in first and then fold the T-shirt from bottom to top.

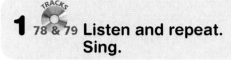 **1** 78 & 79 **Listen and repeat. Sing.**

Introduce the vocabulary

- If possible, use doll's clothes to introduce the clothes vocabulary. If you do not have any, use old, clean children's clothes or baby clothes. You need shoes, socks, trousers, a skirt and a T-shirt.

- Take a teddy or a doll and say *Come on, Teddy, it's time to get dressed.* Get Horsey to help you. Lay all the clothes neatly on a table and say *Horsey, give me the T-shirt, please.* Put the T-shirt on Teddy. Then say *Give me the trousers, please.* Continue until Teddy is fully dressed.

- Then take off the clothes and repeat the activity, asking the children to hand you clothes. Of course they will not remember all the words straight away, so just point to them as you say the words.

- Hold up clothes flashcards and say the words clearly. Give each one to a child and help them to come up to the front and put the flashcards next to the item of clothing.

Use the book

- Help the children open their books at page 49.

- Explain that Lily and Jack are dressing a doll and a teddy. Let the children point and say the clothes words they have remembered.

Play the CD

- Play the recording and encourage the children to repeat.

 TRACK 78

shoes
socks
trousers
skirt
T-shirt

- Now look at the clothes again. Ask questions in L1, e.g. What colour are Teddy's trousers? What about the doll's skirt?

Play the song

- Play the CD and encourage the children to join in.
- Play the song again and point to your clothes as you sing and dance.

 TRACK 79

Look at me, look at me!
Look at me, look at me!
A T-shirt, skirt
Shoes and socks!
A T-shirt, skirt
Shoes and socks!

Look at me, look at me!
Look at me, look at me!
A T-shirt, trousers
Shoes and socks!
A T-shirt, trousers
Shoes and socks!

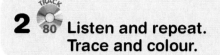 **2** 80 **Listen and repeat. Trace and colour.**

Introduce the letter *u*

- Show the flashcard of the letter *u* and say the sound. Write it on the board several times, saying the sound each time. Write other letters around these and let the children come and circle them as you say the different sounds.

- See pages 20 and 45 for more letter games.

Game Play *Alphabet balloons.*

- Write letters with a marker pen on uninflated balloons. The children can help you with this. Blow the balloons up; the children will enjoy watching the letters get bigger. Tie the balloons and toss them around. When the children catch a balloon, prompt them to say the sound of the letter written on it. Throw several up in the air at the same time and call out a sound. The children try to catch the correct balloon.

- If possible, have a real umbrella to show the children. If not, hold up the flashcard of an umbrella and say *umbrella.*

Craft **Make umbrellas.**

- Have a pack of coloured cupcake paper cases. Cut them in half. Help the children to glue them onto paper. Either add a handle made from a pipe cleaner or a piece of card, or draw handles. The children could paint rainy sky pictures with cotton wool clouds and add their paper umbrellas to the background. Add blue glitter for rain (see teacher's website, http://www.macmillanyounglearners.com/learningstars/teacher).

Use the book

- Show the children that Horsey has a new letter on his necklace today. Say the sound of the letter. Point to the umbrella and say *umbrella*. Say /ʌ/, /ʌ/, /ʌ/, *umbrella*.

Play the CD

- Play the recording and encourage the children to repeat.

TRACK 80

> *u umbrella*
> *u u u u u*
> *umbrella*

- Help the children to trace the letter *u* and colour the umbrella.

Unit 7 Lesson 2

Lesson aims

- To become familiar with the routine of taking your shoes off at home and putting them on again before you go out.

- To learn the sound of the letter *v* and associate it with *van*.

Materials: shoe-shapes from coloured card, shoelaces or ribbons (see teacher's website); a doll with shoes, doll or baby socks or slippers; a toy van (optional); paper plates, strips of stiff card, paint, paintbrushes, stickers (optional) (see teacher's website); a real car key or one made from card (optional)

Warm up

- Do a shoe-lacing activity to help develop the children's fine motor skills (see teacher's website, http://www.macmillanyounglearners.com/learningstars/teacher).

- Make shoe-shapes from coloured card. Punch holes into them and give the children shoelaces or ribbons to thread from one side to the other. Most children will find this activity challenging enough. If, however, they can do it easily, show them how to tie a simple knot too.

1 TRACK 81 **Match. Sing.**

Introduce the routine

- Use a doll with shoes to demonstrate this activity. Take the doll outside and say *Come in, Dolly*. When she is in the classroom, say *Take your shoes off, please*. Take the doll's shoes off and lay them neatly to one side. Then put socks or little slippers on her feet. If you do not have any small enough, use a pair of clean baby socks for this.

- Let the doll play indoors for a while and then say *Let's go out, Dolly. Put your shoes on, please*. Change the doll's socks or slippers for her shoes and take her outside the classroom again.

Use the book

- Help the children open their books at page 50.

- Look at the pictures together. Point to the first picture and ask if the boy is coming in or going out of the house. Then ask if he has taken his shoes off or put them on. Repeat with the second picture.

- Then look at the pictures underneath and say *shoes, socks*. Give the children time to decide which one goes with each picture above (i.e. first picture – socks, second picture – shoes). Help them match the shoes/socks to the correct picture by drawing a matching line.

Play the song

- Play the CD and encourage the children to join in.

- You can mime the actions as you sing along with the CD.

- It might be too tricky for the children to actually take their shoes on and off as they sing, but once they have learnt the song, you can sing it more slowly and let them do the actions.

TRACK 81

> *Take your shoes off, take your shoes off*
> *Take your shoes off, please.*
>
> *Put your shoes on, put your shoes on*
> *Put your shoes on, please.*

2 TRACK 82 Listen and repeat. Trace and colour.

Introduce the letter *v*

- Show the flashcard of the letter *v* and say the sound. Write it on the board several times, saying the sound each time. Show the children that it is a nice easy letter to write – down and then up again. Say *Down, up!* as you write. Let them have fun trying to write it with you or tracing over the letters you have written.

- If you have a toy van, show that. If not, show the flashcard and say *Van. It's a van.* Children are often very observant about the differences in vehicles and they might be able to tell you what the difference is between a van and a car. We can put lots of things in vans and people usually use them for work.

- See pages 20 and 45 for more letter games.

Craft Make steering wheels.

- Cut the centres out of paper plates. Cut strips of stiff card and help the children glue them together in a T-shape to make the centres of the steering wheels. Glue the centres to the rims of the plates. Now let the children paint the whole steering wheel. They do not need to be black like ordinary steering wheels – the children can choose any colour and add stickers too (see teacher's website, http://www.macmillanyounglearners.com/learningstars/teacher).

 Tip It is a good idea to assign chores to children to encourage their sense of responsibility and confidence in their ability to do things. Making children responsible for tidying up the materials used in the craft activities is a great opportunity to do this.

Act out Put on your seat belt.

- Put two chairs together as if you are in the front seats of a van. Ask them which side the driver sits in. Let the children work that out and then give the 'driver' the steering wheel. Before they 'go' anywhere, they must put on their seat belts! Mime pulling the seat belt over and clicking it in. Now the driver can start the car. You could give the driver a real car key, or you could make one from card. Encourage them to all make driving noises as the children go somewhere in their van.

Use the book

- Show the children that Horsey has a new letter on his necklace today and help them to say the sound. Point to the van and say *van*. Then say /v/, /v/, /v/, *van*.

Play the CD

- Play the recording and encourage the children to repeat.

 TRACK 82

v van

v v v v

van

- Help the children to trace the letter *v* and colour the van.

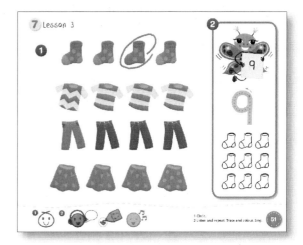

Lesson aims

- To circle the odd one out in a series of four pictures.

- To review colours and shapes, and the clothes: *socks, T-shirt, trousers* and *skirt*.

- To learn the number *9* and become aware of the amount.

Materials: different coloured play bricks; real clothes, e.g. two pairs of socks of different colours (optional); ten items, e.g. toy cars, bags

Warm up

- Make patterns with different coloured play bricks. Make Horsey line up one red, one yellow, one red, one yellow brick and let the children join in with him and help find the correct colour bricks to continue the pattern.

- Make the patterns more complicated, e.g. add other items to make sequences: red brick, yellow brick, green crayon. Keep the work focused on patterns and not just playing with the bricks. Let them have some time to build or play as they wish in the break.

1 Circle.

Introduce the activity

- If possible, use real clothes for this introduction, e.g. two pairs of socks of different colours. Put down one blue sock, one yellow and one more blue. Then ask the children to point to the one that is different. Let the children take that one away. Continue with different clothes and colours.

Use the book

- Help the children open their books at page 51.
- Ask the children to look at the first row of pictures. Show them that one sock has been circled. Ask them if they know why. If necessary, point to each picture and say *circles, circles, squares, circles.* Ask them to trace the sample circle for practice.
- Continue with the other rows. Encourage them to say the names of the clothes and the colours too.

  Answers: Row 1: the sock with the squares, Row 2: the T-shirt with wavy lines, Row 3: the blue trousers, Row 4: the skirt with the circles

2 83 & 84 Listen and repeat. Trace and colour. Sing.

Introduce the number 9

- Show the flashcard for the number *9* and write it on the board several times, saying *nine* as you do so. Hold up nine fingers. Put ten items on a table and ask Horsey and then the children to bring you nine of them. Say, for example, *Nine cars, please.* Give them bags to put them in if they cannot carry all of them.
- See ideas for more number games on pages 22 and 32.

Use the book

- Show the children that Bella has a new number today and ask them to point and say *nine.* Count the socks together.

Play the CD

- Play the recording and encourage the children to repeat.

TRACK 83   *Nine* [pause] *nine* [pause] *nine* [pause]

- Then help the children to trace the number *9* and colour the socks.

Play the song

- Play the CD and encourage the children to join in.

TRACK 84
1 2 3 4 5 6 7 8 9
How are you today?
I'm fine!
[repeat]

- Line up in two rows as you sing. Dance towards each other and shake hands as you sing *How are you today? I'm fine!*
- You could also dance around the class and encourage the children to shake hands with whoever they meet when they come to saying the greetings.

Unit 7 Lesson 4

Lesson aims

- To listen to a story which reviews the language of the unit.
- To act out a version of the story.

Materials: dressed dolls, a cloth, a blanket (optional); wooden clothes pegs, a length of string, doll or baby clothes; bowls of water, soap powder, old clothes to wash (optional)

Warm up

- 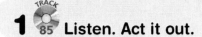 Play a colour observation game. Take a dressed doll and hold it up. Then cover her up with a cloth and ask the children *What colour is her skirt?* or *What colour are her shoes?* See if they can remember and call out the colours. Continue with other dolls. You could wrap yourself up in a blanket and ask them *What colour is my skirt?* As they get used to the game, they will become more observant.

1 TRACK 85 Listen. Act it out.

Introduce the activity

- 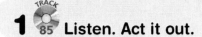 Play a washing line game. Give the children some wooden clothes pegs and show them how they open and close. Tie a length of string to two chairs to make a clothes line in the classroom. Help them peg dolls or babies clothes to the line.

Use the book

- Help the children open their books at page 52.
- If necessary, explain that in this story, Jack and Lily are pegging their clothes on the line, but Horsey accidentally splashes Jack's white T-shirt with strawberry juice. Horsey then washes it again.

- Let the children look at the pictures and point and say the names of the clothes Jack and Lily have got. Ask them to name the colours too.

Play the CD

- Play the recording several times while the children just listen.

 TRACK 85

Jack: *My trousers.*
Lily: *My skirt and my socks.*

Jack: *My T-shirt.*
Horsey: *It's white.*
Jack: *Yes, Horsey. My T-shirt's white.*

Lily: *Horsey!*
Jack: *Oh no! My T-shirt's red!*

Horsey: *Sorry, Jack!*
Jack: *Thank you, Horsey!*

Act it out.

- If possible, let the children play at washing clothes in the playground. Give the children bowls of water and let them add a little soap powder and swish it around to make bubbles. Give them old clothes to wash. Show them how to rinse the clothes in clean water afterwards and let them have fun wringing them out – they might like to do this is pairs with one child twisting the garment one way and the other child twisting in the opposite direction.
- You probably will not want to act out Horsey staining a white T-shirt red, but you could mime the story and act out Jack and Lily's surprise when it happens and Horsey feeling sorry for his actions.

Lesson aims

- To develop cognitive skills by matching children to their shoes and possessions.
- To learn the sound of the letter *w* and associate it with *window*.

Materials: sheets of paper (one for each child), strips of card, pieces of material for curtains (optional), sticks or straws (optional) (see teacher's website)

Warm up

- Hold up a pair of shoes and say *shoes*. Prompt the children to repeat. Hold up a school bag, say *bag* and the children repeat.
- Encourage the children to point to their own shoes or school bag and say *(My) shoes* or *(My) bag*.

87

1 Match.

Introduce the activity

 Play _The going to school race._

- This game is best done outside in the playground. If you do not have an outside area, you can clear a space in the classroom. With the children, decide which things they need to get ready for school. Do they come to school in their pyjamas or do they need their school uniform? What about a bag and a lunchbox?

- Now make lines of some of these objects. Lay a child's coat or top on the floor. Then leave a space and put down a school bag. Then leave another gap and put down a lunchbox. Make one line of objects for each child playing the game.

- The children line up as if for a race; if you have limited space, they can race in twos or threes. Say _One, two, three, go!_ and they run to the coat and put it on, then run to the bag and pick it up, then to the lunchbox and put it in their bag. Finally, they run to the finishing line.

Use the book

- Help the children open their books at page 53.

- Let the children point and name the items, _shoes, bag._

- Give them time to decide which items belong to which child. Help them to draw matching lines.

  Answers: Boy: the blue shoes and bag, Girl: the red shoes and bag

2 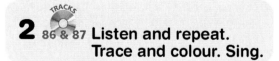 86 & 87 Listen and repeat. Trace and colour. Sing.

Introduce the letter _w_

- Show the flashcard of the letter _w_ and say the sound. Write it on the board several times, saying the sound each time. Now write the letter _v_ again. Point out that _w_ looks like two _vs_ together. Let them have fun trying to draw the letter _w_ on the board.

- Show the flashcard of a window and say _window._ Point to the classroom window and say _window._ Ask them what they can see out of this window, and what they can see from their bedroom window. Ask if they can see trees or houses or cars, and if they can see the sky, etc.

- See pages 20 and 45 for more letter games.

 Make windows.

- Give the children sheets of paper and help them to draw what they want to see from their windows. Give them strips of card and help them to paste these over and around the pictures to make window frames. You could add curtains. Cut pieces of material and poke some holes in the top. Thread them through sticks or straws and paste them along the top of the frame (see teacher's website, http://www.macmillanyounglearners.com/learningstars/teacher).

Use the book

- Show the children that Horsey has a new letter on his necklace and help them to say the sound. Point to the window and say _window._ Then say /w/, /w/, /w/, _window._

Play the CD

- Play the recording and encourage the children to repeat.

86   _w window_
_w w w w_
window

- Help the children to trace the letter _w_ and colour the window.

Play the song

- Sing the _Alphabet_ song up to _t._ Tell the children they are going to sing three more names of letters today: _u, v, w._ Tell them that they have nearly learnt to sing the whole English alphabet – only three more letters to go and they will know it all!

- Play the CD and encourage the children to join in.

- See page 25 for Teacher's notes on playing the _Eat the letter_ game.

87   _a b c_
_d e f_
_g h i_
_j k l_
_m n o p_
_q r s t_
_u v w_

Unit 7 Lesson 6

Lesson aim

- To recognise the difference between the emotions happy and sad.

Materials: a doll, a teddy, wrapping paper, gifts, e.g. toy cars, sticky tape; paper plates (one for each child)

Warm up

- Make presents for a doll and teddy. Give the children some small pieces of wrapping paper and help them to wrap up gifts such as books or cars or crayons. They will need help wrapping the paper, but they will enjoy putting the sticky tape on. Give the presents to the toys and say *It's for you!* Make the toys say *Thank you!*

1 Colour.

Introduce the topic

- Use Horsey puppet or a doll or teddy. Horsey always looks smiling and happy, but you can make him pretend to be sad by changing your own facial expression and making him hide his face in your shoulder. You could pretend that Horsey is sad because he cannot find his school bag or his favourite book or because Teddy will not play with him. Say *What's the matter, Horsey?* and make him shake his head. Say *Are you sad, Horsey?* and make him nod his head.

- Encourage the children to try to cheer Horsey up and make him happy, e.g. help him find his bag or book or play with Teddy. Make Horsey look happy again. Say *Oh, Horsey, you're happy. Horsey is happy!*

Craft Make happy and sad faces.

- Give the children paper plates and help them to draw happy and sad faces on the back and front. If they are feeling happy, they hold up the happy face and if they are sad they turn the plate around.

Use the book

- Help the children open their books at page 54.

- Look at the photos at the top. Ask in L1: Which one is happy and which is sad? Help the children to point and say.

- Now look at the big picture together. Point to each child and say *Happy or sad?* Prompt the child to say *happy* or *sad* as appropriate.

- Give the children red crayons and tell them to colour the stars next to the children who are happy. Then give them blue crayons and ask them to colour the stars next to the children who are sad.

  Answers: child 1 and child 2 are happy, child 3 and child 4 are sad

Unit 7 Lesson 7

Lesson aims

- To match patterns and review clothes vocabulary.

- To make paper dolls.

- To learn the colour *black* and become aware of the shape *diamond*.

Materials: card shapes of triangles, squares, circles and rectangles, a picture by the artist Mondrian, coloured squares and rectangles (optional), thick black marker pens (optional), rulers (optional); old pieces of material or sheets of coloured and patterned wrapping paper cut into squares (two of each with the same pattern and colours), a rug on the floor (optional); card outlines of dolls (see teacher's website), wool or strips of paper for hair, scraps of material or coloured wrapping paper; a picture of a bat (optional); a square piece of card, diamond shaped cards in different colours, shiny foil, glitter, stickers

Warm up

- Give the children small card shapes of triangles, squares, circles and rectangles and help them to draw around them onto paper. They do not have to be drawn separately, they can overlap.

- Find a picture by the artist Mondrian to show them. Ask questions in L1, e.g. What colours can you see? What about the shapes? If the children like his paintings you could help them to make some with coloured squares and rectangles and thick black marker pens. They might like to draw lines with a ruler. Help them by holding the ruler in place as they draw.

1 Match.

Introduce the activity

- Take some old pieces of material into the class. These could be from clothes which are no longer needed or scraps of material. If you do not have access to scraps then use different sheets of coloured and patterned wrapping paper.

- Cut squares of material or paper so that there are at least two of each with the same pattern and colours. Place them all over a table or on a rug on the floor and let the children find matching pieces and bring them to you. Say *Yes, they're the same.* or *No, they aren't the same.*

Use the book

- Help the children open their books at page 55.

- Let them point and say the clothes they can see and then work out which T-shirt belongs to which child, according to the patterns.

- Help them to draw matching lines (i.e. from the boy to the green T-shirt and from the girl to the pink T-shirt).

Craft. Make paper dolls.

- Give the children large, simple card outlines of dolls (see template on the teacher's website, http://www.macmillanyounglearners.com/learningstars/teacher). Help them to draw faces and stick on wool or strips of paper for hair. Cut clothes for the dolls from scraps of material or coloured wrapping paper. Let the children choose how they want to dress their dolls and then stick the clothes onto the card dolls.

2 88 & 89 Listen and repeat. Colour. Sing.

Introduce the colour *black*

- Show the flashcard of the colour *black* and say *black*. Ask the children to point to things in the classroom which are black. What about their shoes, or the pupils of their eyes?

- Show a picture or flashcard of a bat. Elicit the name and ask if the children can remember if it is awake in the day or the night.

Introduce the shape *diamond*

- Show the flashcard of the diamond shape and say *diamond*. Turn a square piece of card so that it is a diamond shape.

- You could make 'diamond' necklaces with different coloured cards strung together. Stick shiny foil, glitter and stickers to the card shapes too.

Use the book

- Point to the diamond shape next to the tent. Say *black*. Draw a diamond with your finger. Say *Diamond. A black diamond.*

- Ask the children to open their books at pages 2 and 3 and see if they can find the same diamond shape in Lessons 1 and 2.

- Point to the bat and say *bat*.

Play the CD

- Play the recording and encourage the children to repeat.

TRACK 88

Black, black, black
Bat! Bat!

- Help the children to colour the bat black. Ask the children to name other things which are black, e.g. coal, dogs.

- Have the children look and point to things that are diamonds in the classroom.

Play the song

- Play the CD and encourage the children to join in.

- Play the song again and the children mime swooping and flying like bats as they sing.

- Finish off the unit by demonstrating the Bat yoga pose (see teacher's website) and encourage the children to join in.

TRACK 89

Black, black, black,
Black, black, black,
Bat! Bat!
Black, black, black.

Unit 8 Home

By the end of Unit 8 the children will be able to:

- say the words for rooms: *bedroom, bathroom, kitchen, living room.*
- say where they are: *I'm in the (bedroom).*
- show an appreciation of their own homes.
- say the sounds, sing the names and trace the letters *x*, *y* and *z*.
- recognise that *fox* goes with *x*, *yo-yo* with *y* and *zebra* with *z*.
- sing the complete *Alphabet* song.
- recognise and say the number *10* and understand the amount.
- distinguish between hot and cold.
- make an alphabet necklace.
- review vocabulary, letters, shapes, numbers and colours from previous units.

New/Reviewed words and language

bedroom, bathroom, kitchen, living room
I'm in the (bedroom).
/ks/, /j/, /z/, *x, y, z*
fox, yo-yo, zebra
10, ten
hot, cold

Classroom language

Can you find the …?
Where are you?
I don't know!

Value of the unit

I like my home.

Materials

card, paper, glue, scissors, crayons, pencils,
a hole punch
Horsey puppet
flashcards
CD

Unit 8 Lesson 1

Lesson aims

- To learn and say the rooms: *bedroom, bathroom, kitchen, living room.*
- To learn to appreciate their own homes.

Materials: bricks or boxes, dolls and teddies, toy cars (optional), card trees (optional), strips of grey card (optional); clothes lines or string, sheets or tablecloths, pegs, shoeboxes, play food, paper plates, plastic cutlery, a bowl of water, a bar of soap, material (optional), photographs of the different rooms of the house (optional)

Warm up

- Play with bricks or boxes and help the children to make houses for Horsey and the dolls and teddies. You could make a whole little village of houses and add cars and card trees outside. Lay down strips of grey card to make roads around the houses.

1 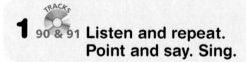 **90 & 91 Listen and repeat. Point and say. Sing.**

Introduce the vocabulary

- Hold up the flashcards of the rooms and say the words clearly.

- Bring clothes lines or string, clean old sheets or tablecloths and pegs to the classroom. If you have made a *Learning Stars* tent in the corner, tell the children that today you are going to make it much bigger. Attach the string or clothes lines to chairs and tables and, with the help of the children, peg the cloths to the lines so that you make extra 'rooms' in your tent.

- Put some of the dolls in shoebox beds in one room. Say *Shhh, the dolls are asleep.* and mime sleeping. Ask them what they think that room is. Say *Yes, it's the bedroom!*

- Put a little table and chair in another of the 'rooms' and let the children help you to lay the table for dinner. They can use play food and paper plates and plastic cutlery. Put some teddies on the chair. Ask what they think this room is. Say *It's the kitchen!*

- Put a bowl with some water and soap in another room and put a dolly in the bath. Say *It's the bathroom!*

- Finally, put some chairs and books and toys in the fourth room. You could cover the chairs with some material to make them look like comfortable armchairs or sofas. Say *This is the living room.*

- You could take in photographs of the different rooms to show the children.

 Play with Horsey puppet. Put him in different rooms. Say *Where are you, Horsey?* and make him say *I'm in the bathroom!* Then let the children play this game and hide in different rooms.

- Get Horsey to say *This is my home. I like my home!* Ask the children which rooms they have in their own homes. Then ask if they like their own homes and encourage them to say *Yes!*

Use the book

- Help the children open their books at pages 56 and 57.

- Let the children look and decide which room is which.

Play the CD

- Play the recording and encourage the children to repeat.

 90
bedroom
bathroom
kitchen
living room

- Point and say the rooms together. Ask the children *Where's Jack?* and encourage them to point to the bedroom and say *bedroom.* Repeat with: *Where's Lily?* (in the bathroom) *Where's Horsey?* (in the kitchen) *Where's Bella?* (in the living room).

Play the song

- Play the CD and encourage the children to join in.

91
I'm in the bedroom, the bedroom, the bedroom.
I'm in the bedroom. Hooray!
I'm in the kitchen, the kitchen, the kitchen.
I'm in the kitchen. Hooray!
I'm in the living room, the living room, the living room.
I'm in the living room. Hooray!
I'm in the bathroom, the bathroom, the bathroom.
I'm in the bathroom. Hooray!

- Go from room to room in your playhouse as you sing this song together. If you have not been able to make the playhouse, you can mime actions for each room: sleeping in the bedroom, cooking in the kitchen, reading or drawing in the living room and washing in the bathroom.

Unit 8 Lesson 2

Lesson aim

- To review vocabulary, colours, shapes and letters.

Materials: four boxes, playdough or plasticine (see teacher's website)

Warm up

- Make a bedroom, kitchen, living room and bathroom using boxes (see teacher's website, http://www.macmillanyounglearners.com/learningstars/teacher). Let the children have fun making the furniture for each room out of playdough or plasticine and designing their 'house'.

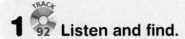 **1** **Listen and find.**

Introduce the activity

- Put the following vocabulary flashcards on one table: grapes, apple, teddy, ball, doll, crayon, book, cat, rabbit.

- Put the shape flashcards on another table: square, triangle, circle, rectangle, diamond.
- Place the alphabet flashcards on another table.
- Place the colour flashcards on another table: red, yellow, green, blue, white, black.
- As you lay these cards out, encourage the children to name them and to say the sounds of the letters.

Use the book

- Help the children open their books at pages 56 and 57.
- Hold up one of the alphabet flashcards. Say, e.g. *Can you find the letter (a)?* and show the *a* flashcard. Let the children look at their books and find the letter *a*. Continue with the other letters, shapes and colours.

Play the CD

- Play the recording and encourage the children to listen and repeat.
- Play the CD again. Pause after each item and give the children time to find and point to the picture in their books.

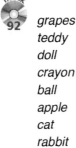
grapes
teddy
doll
crayon
ball
apple
cat
rabbit
book

There are lots of words and letters to review in this lesson so you might like to do this activity in two separate sessions.

Unit 8 Lesson 3

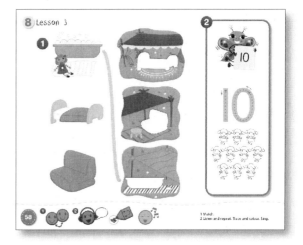

Lesson aims

- To match furniture to shapes in rooms and review room vocabulary.
- To learn the number *10* and become aware of the amount.

Materials: music; pictures of a sofa, bed and bath (optional); chalk; ten skittles (or empty tin cans or small boxes), soft balls; cake and ten candles (optional)

Warm up

- **Game** Play a *Tidy up musical statues* game. Tell the children that you are all going to tidy up the classroom whilst listening to some nice music. When the music stops, you all have to freeze and stand still like statues. Then start the music and continue clearing up again. Give the children specific tasks, like sorting the cars into one box, putting the big books on a shelf and so on.

1 Match.

Introduce the activity

- Use pictures or the 'furniture' you made for the big playhouse to present the words *sofa*, *bed* and *bath*. Make Horsey sit on the sofa and say *Horsey's on the sofa*. Put him in the 'shoebox bed' and say *Horsey's in bed*. Then put him in the plastic bath and say *Horsey's in the bath*.

Use the book

- Help the children open their books at page 58.
- Let the children point and say which rooms they can see (bedroom, living room and bathroom).
- Look at the furniture on the left and say *bath*, *bed* and *sofa*. Ask them where they think these things should go. Help them to trace over the sample line; then ask them to draw lines to match the other furniture to the rooms.

2 93 & 94 Listen and repeat. Trace and colour. Sing.

Introduce the number 10

- Show the flashcard with the number *10* and say *ten*. Write it on the board several times. Ask what the children notice about this number. (There are two numbers to write now.) Show them that they are both easy to write.
- Hold up ten fingers and get them to do the same. Put different items on the table and ask them to bring you ten of them. Count them out together as they do so.
- See ideas for more number games on pages 22 and 32.

Game Play *Hopping and jumping games*.

- Ask the children to hop or jump while you count up to ten. See if they can hop five times on one leg and five times on the other.
- In the playground write the numbers *1–10* inside large chalk circles. Call out a number and the children run and jump into that circle.
- Play skittle games, e.g. line up ten skittles (or empty tin cans, or boxes) and give the children soft balls and see how many they can knock over by rolling the ball.

Use the book

- Ask the children what number Bella has got today. Help the children point to it and say *ten*. Count the dolls together.

Play the CD

- Play the recording and encourage the children to repeat.

TRACK 93

Ten [pause] *ten* [pause] *ten* [pause] *ten* [pause]

- Help the children trace the number *10* and colour the dolls.

Play the song

- Play the CD and encourage the children to join in.
- Play the song again and encourage the children to dance and hold up the correct number of fingers as they sing the complete *Numbers* song.

TRACK 94

1 2 3 4 5 6 7 8 9 10
[repeat]

- Celebrate with the children when you have sung this song. Now they can sing all the numbers from *1–10*. You could bring in a cake and let the children help you put ten candles on it.

8 Lesson 4

1 Listen. Act it out. 59

Lesson aims

- To listen to a story which reviews the language of the unit.
- To act out a version of the story.

Materials: a large piece of paper, a card roof, shapes of squares and rectangles, pictures of furniture cut from magazines; a scarf; a small doll, a cloth

Warm up

- Work together to make a large picture of a house. Divide a piece of paper into four rooms and add a card roof. Let the children decide which rooms should be the bathroom, kitchen, living room and bedroom. Give the children shapes of squares and rectangles and let them decide what they could be, e.g. a square could be a table, a rectangle could be a bed. Help them to paste them in the correct rooms. Add pictures cut from magazines of other pieces of furniture.

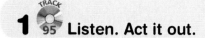

1 95 Listen. Act it out.

Introduce the activity

- Play with Horsey puppet in the playhouse again. This time cover Horsey's eyes with a scarf as a loose blindfold. Put Horsey in one room and say *Where are you, Horsey?* Make him say *I don't know!* Prompt the children to tell him where he is.

- Now you walk into one of the rooms. Close your eyes and make Horsey ask you *Where are you?* Say *I don't know, Horsey.* Then make Horsey say *In the bathroom!*

- Let the children play too, but hold their hands as they close their eyes and walk into a room. Do not make anyone play who is frightened of doing so.

Use the book

- Help the children open their books at page 59.

- If necessary, explain that Horsey has got into a muddle with one of the sheets in the play tent and does not know where he is.

Play the CD

- Play the recording several times while the children just listen.

---

95 **Jack:** *Horsey! Where are you?*
Horsey: *I don't know!*

Lily: *In the living room?*
Bella: *No!*
Lily and Jack: *Where are you, Horsey?*
Horsey: *I don't know!*

Jack: *In the bathroom?*
Bella: *No!*
Lily and Jack: *Where are you, Horsey?*
Horsey: *I don't know!*

Lily: *Horsey! You're in the bedroom!*
Horsey: *Oh yes! Thank you!*

Act it out.

- Now act out a version of the story. You could use the large drawing of the house. Lay it on a table. Put a small doll in one of the rooms and cover her with a cloth. Help the children to act out the dialogue, using words and phrases they remember as they ask the doll where she is.

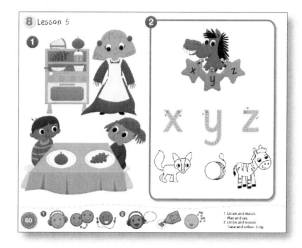

8 Lesson 5

1 2

x y z

60 1. Listen and match. Play and say. 2. Listen and repeat. Trace and colour. Sing.

Lesson aims

- To listen to a dialogue of children play-acting in the kitchen.

95

- To match shapes to food items.
- To do a role-play based on the dialogue and the scene in the book.
- To learn the sounds of the letters *x*, *y* and *z* and to associate them with *fox*, *yo-yo* and *zebra*.
- To sing the complete *Alphabet* song.

Materials: dressing-up clothes or old sheets and tablecloths, paper beards and moustaches (optional), scarves (optional); a big doll, a scrap of material, play food, paper plates (one for Horsey and one for each child); sand trays or trays of lentils; a toy yo-yo; zebra shapes (one for each child), black and white strips of paper, a thick black marker (optional)

Warm up

- 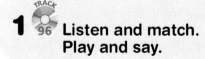 Play dressing-up games and pretend to be members of a family. Bring in clean, old clothes for the dressing-up box or old sheets and tablecloths if you do not have any old clothes. You could make paper beards and moustaches and girls could wear scarves to make their hair longer. Encourage the children to say *I'm Dad. I'm Mum. I'm Grandpa. I'm Grandma.* Help them to think of ways that their parents do and say things – children are often very good at imitating others.

1 🔊 96 Listen and match. Play and say.

Introduce the activity

- Take a big doll and make an apron for her to wear from a scrap of material. Make her say *Hello, I'm Mum.*

- Give the doll play food. Give Horsey a paper plate. Make Horsey say *Mum, a tomato, please.* Make the doll give Horsey a tomato. Make him say *Thank you!*
- Give the children paper plates. Then let the children take turns to ask the doll for food.

Use the book

- Help the children open their books at page 60.
- Ask them to say what they can see in the picture. Encourage them to point and name the food items at the top.
- Then ask them what they think the children in the picture are saying. Encourage them to point and say what they think.

Play the CD

- Play the recording and encourage the children to listen to the dialogue.

🔊 96

Girl 1: *I'm Mum. I'm in the kitchen.*
Girl 2: *Mum, grapes, please!*
Girl 1: *Grapes!*
Girl 2: *Thank you.*
Boy: *Mum, a tomato, please!*
Girl 1: *A tomato!*
Boy: *Thank you.*

- Now help the children to draw lines to match the pictures of a tomato and grapes to the shapes on the plates.

- Play the CD once more and then let the children play this game together. If possible, put them into groups of three: Mum and two children. Then give them props such as paper plates and toy food. Encourage them to use the language from the dialogue when they can, e.g. *Mum, a cake, please! A cake! Thank you.* Alternatively, play as a class with you taking the role of Mum and the children taking turns to be the children.

2 🔊 97 & 98 Listen and repeat. Trace and colour. Sing.

Introduce the letter *x*

- Show the flashcard of the letter *x* and say the sound. Write it on the board several times, saying the sound as you do so. Show the children that this is a nice easy letter to write. Give them sand trays or trays of lentils and let them have fun writing the letter.
- Show the flashcard of a fox. Prompt them to remember the name and then ask what they know about foxes in L1, e.g. Do they sleep at night or are they awake then? Say *fox* and ask them if they think the /ks/ sound comes at the beginning or the end of the word.

Introduce the letter *y*

- Show the flashcard of the letter *y* and say the sound. Write it on the board several times, saying the sound as you do so. Write lots of letters on the board around them and get the children to come up to the board and point as you say the sounds.
- Show the flashcard of a yo-yo and say *yo-yo*. Show the children a toy yo-yo and say *yo-yo*. Ask if anyone can make a yo-yo work. It is rather tricky for young children, but let them try.

Introduce the letter z

- Show the flashcard of the letter *z* and say the sound. Write it on the board several times, saying the sound as you do so.

 Show the flashcard of the zebra and say *zebra*. Ask questions in L1, e.g. What colour are zebras? They look a bit like horses, but they are black and white. You could make black and white stripes from paper and cover Horsey with them. Make him say *Look, I'm a zebra!*

- See pages 20 and 45 for more letter games.

Make zebras.

- Give the children zebra shapes to cover with black and white strips. They could use a thick black marker for this, but make sure it is not an indelible pen.

Use the book

- Now look at the book and show the children that Horsey has three different letters on his necklace today. Point and say the sounds /ks/, /j/, /z/.
- Then point to the fox and say *fox*. Say /ks/, /ks/, /ks/, *fox*. Then point to the yo-yo and say *yo-yo*. Say /j/, /j/, /j/, *yo-yo*. Then point to the zebra and say *zebra*. Say /z/, /z/, /z/, *zebra*.

Play the CD

- Play the recording and encourage the children to repeat.

97

x fox

x x x x

fox

---

y yo-yo

y y y y

yo-yo

z zebra

z z z z

zebra

- Help the children to trace the letters *x*, *y* and *z* and colour the fox, yo-yo and zebra.

Play the song

- Remind them that the letters of the alphabet also have names. Point to the letter flashcards and say *x*, *y* and *z*.
- Now tell the children they know all the sounds of the English alphabet and all the names and so can now sing the whole *Alphabet* song.
- Play the CD and encourage the children to join in.
- See page 25 for Teacher's notes on playing the *Eat the letter* game.

98

a b c

d e f

g h i

j k l

m n o p

q r s t

u v w

x y z

- Celebrate with the children when they have sung the song and make sure they feel really good about their achievements.

Lesson aims

- To become aware of which things are hot and which are cold.
- To say *hot* and *cold*.

Materials: ice cube trays, bowls, jugs of water, small plastic glasses (one for each child), juice; a red and a blue label, two plastic bottles, hot (not boiling) water, iced water

Warm up

- Fill ice cube trays. Put ice cube trays into bowls and give the children jugs of water. Let them pour water slowly into the trays. Tell them to try not to pour too quickly so that the water does not flow out. When they have filled them, take them carefully to the school kitchen and let the children watch you put them in the freezer. Later in the day you can all go and see what has happened to the water and have nice iced juice.

1 Point and say. Colour.

Introduce the topic

- Put red and blue labels on two plastic bottles. Fill the red one with hot (not boiling) water and the blue one with iced water. Put the tops on both bottles. Give the hot one to the children, one by one and let them touch it. Say *Hot! It's hot.* Then take the cold one around the class and let the children touch that. Say *Cold! It's cold.*

 Mime hot and cold.

- Mime drinking hot drinks: you cannot drink it quickly, you have to be careful and sip it and you must be careful not to spill it too.
- Now mime drinking a cold drink or eating an ice cream: sometimes they make you shiver because they are so cold and your mouth feels funny.

Use the book

- Help the children open their books at page 61.
- Let the children look at the photos at the top of the page and decide which they think is the hot drink and which is the cold one. Point to the cup of hot chocolate and say *hot.* Then point to the glass of iced water and say *cold.*
- Then look at the main picture together and decide which things are hot and which are cold. Help them to colour the stars next to the hot things red and the stars next to the cold things blue.

  Answers: Red stars: the bread and the mug with the hot drink, Blue stars: the ice cream and the iced drink

Unit 8 Lesson 7

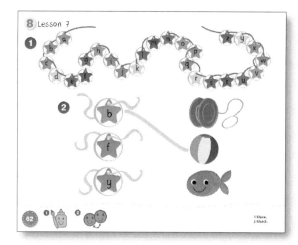

Lesson aims

- To make alphabet necklaces.
- To match letters to pictures.

Materials: letter cards (optional); card shapes: squares, triangles, circles, rectangles, clouds and diamonds, glitter, cord or ribbon

Warm up

- Go back through the Pupil's Book and ask the children to find all the pictures of Horsey wearing his alphabet necklace. Encourage them to try to say the sounds of the letters and the words.

- **TRACK 98** Sing the *Alphabet* song again. You could give letter cards to each child and encourage them to hold up their card when they say the letter.

1 Make.

Introduce the activity

- Show the children the flashcard of the alphabet chain. Explain that they are going to make a similar chain each but with their own name. Make card shapes: squares, triangles, circles, rectangles, clouds and diamonds. Make them large enough to write letters on but small enough to be made into name necklaces. Punch holes in the tops of each small card.

- Now write the children's names on the board. The children have not seen capital letters yet, but start each name with a capital letter. Point to each name and say it. When a child hears his or her name, they come up to the front and write the letters for their name on card shapes. Say the names of the letters now, not the sounds, as that is how we spell out names.

- Then let the children trace over the letters and decorate each one, e.g. with colours, glitter, etc.

- When all the children have made the letter cards for their name, help them to string the letters, in the correct order, onto cords or ribbon to make necklaces. Finally, tie the necklaces in loose bows around their necks.

> **Tip** Do not expect the children to be able to spell out their names at this stage. Just have fun making the necklaces and gradually they will recognise their name in English letters. You could also make bracelets instead of necklaces.

Use the book

- Help the children open their books at page 62.
- Look at the alphabet necklace at the top. Point to each letter in turn and encourage the children to say the sound and the name.

2 Match.

Introduce the activity

- Put some alphabet flashcards on one table and the corresponding picture flashcards on another and let the children make pairs, e.g. the letter *q* flashcard and the picture flashcard of a queen.

Use the book

- Let the children look at the letters and pictures and decide which letter matches which picture. Encourage them to say the sounds and the words and help them to trace over the sample line; then ask them to draw matching lines between the other letters and pictures.

  Answers: b – ball, f – fish, y – yo-yo

- Finish off the unit by demonstrating the Fish yoga pose (see teacher's website) and encourage the children to join in.
- See End-of-term activities on page 101.

Lesson aim

- To review the vocabulary of Units 7 and 8.

Warm up

- Have a reflection session with the children about all the things they have done and learnt this year. Which games did they like best? Would they like to play them again? Sing some of the songs again. You could prepare an end-of-year concert and invite some of the older children in the school to come and hear the children sing.

- Thank Horsey for all his help this year. The children could do drawings of Horsey and present them to him. Tell the children how much you admire them for all their hard work and good behaviour. Let them know that you have enjoyed being their teacher.

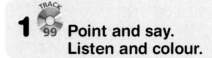

1 99 Point and say. Listen and colour.

Introduce the activity

- Place flashcards of the rooms of the house and clothes vocabulary on the board. Draw a small star next to each one. Remember to place all the pictures low enough for the children to reach them. Let the children come up to the board and point to and say the words.

- Make Horsey call out the words one by one, e.g. *bathroom, shoes*. Let the children come up to the board and colour the stars next to the correct pictures.

Use the book

- Help the children open their books at pages 63 and 64.

- Let the children point and say what they can see.

Play the CD

- Play the recording and encourage the children to listen.

---

 bathroom
shoes
kitchen
trousers
skirt
T-shirt

- Play the CD again. Pause after each word to give the children time to find the matching picture. They then colour the star next to it. Tell the children that if they cannot see the picture on the first page, they will have to turn over the page to look at the pictures on the second page.

End-of-term activities

Mobiles

A good way of reviewing letters and numbers orally is to make a set of the alphabet and numbers to *10* which the children can decorate. Use glitter, sequins, tinsel or any craft materials you have left over from the year, and make them as bright as possible. The children can scrunch tissue paper and stick this on the numbers and letters, as this gives them a 3D effect and is very good for fine motor control and hand-eye coordination. The finished artwork could be hung on wire coat hangers in the classroom or stuck on the wall as part of a corridor display for parents to see.

Messy table

Set up a table where the children can practise direction and emergent writing. Good, cheap things to use include rice, lentils or flour. Also porridge oats if you can get them, as they have a nice silky feel to them. All these things are great to touch and this is a very relaxing way to practise letters and beginning to write in a very stress-free way. Change what is on the table every few days (the flour is likely to be most messy and will need sweeping up every day).

Water 'painting'

One lovely thing to do when the weather is hot is to fill some buckets or bowls with water, take some paintbrushes (the bigger the better, ask in the staffroom if anyone has any old decorating brushes they no longer want and give them a clean) and let the children 'paint' the walls and fences outside. It does not matter if the children get a bit wet – it will cool them down – and the water will soon dry, leaving no mess at all!

Water play

Water play encourages fine motor skills and is also great for maths concepts (more, less, full, empty) as children can fill containers of different sizes. Ideally, use a clean empty sand tray or some bowls and plastic jugs and cups – anything which the children can pour and play with safely. Utensils from your kitchen are also great fun to explore the qualities of water with too, such as sieves and ladles or big spoons.

Playdough

Either use bought playdough or make some home-made playdough – it is very easy and cheap to make and you can put food colouring in it to dye it different colours (see recipe on the teacher's website). Let the children play with the playdough, making whatever they like. (NOTE: it is very important that the children do not eat the home-made playdough, as it has a high salt content.)

Dough letters

Make some dough and give each child a piece, helping and encouraging them to make the shape of the first letter of their name. Let the children knead the dough before forming the letter and then ask them to decorate it with paint, or anything you have in the classroom. Then put them in the oven to bake until hard and the children can take them home. As an extension, you could talk to the children about the change in dough once it has cooked.

Chalk drawing

Let the children draw and practise letters or direction in the playground. Then let them 'tidy up' by sloshing water over the chalk.

Paper cup game

Make some small cards with the *Little Learning Stars* characters on and the first sound in their name.

When you call out *Bella*, two children have to race to find the Bella card and put it in the cup. There are many variations on this game and you can use it very simply to review any vocabulary or letter sounds. Have two children playing at a time and keep the pace quite fast, swapping in other children until everyone has had a turn. This game is a great success with this age group.

Potato printing

This is a nice activity to do outside. Get a long roll of old wallpaper or sugar paper and half-fill a few saucers with paint (too much and they will spill or the potatoes will fall in!) and give the children half a potato each. If you have a theme in mind, such as night animals or trees and flowers, you could draw outlines for the children to fill with the potato prints – they will make great owl 'feathers' or leaves for trees – and ask them to keep in the lines. This activity is great for fine motor skills, revising colours and *Little Learning Stars* topics, while allowing the children to express themselves through art.

Unit by unit assessment sheets

Unit 1

Name	1	2	3	4	5	6	7

1   Recognises the names of the characters in the book: *Jack, Lily, Horsey, Bella.*
2   Can say and understand when to use *Hello* and *Goodbye.*
3   Recognises and uses the commands *Stand up* and *Sit down.*

4   Can say the sounds, sing the names and trace the letters *a*, *b* and *c*.
5   Recognises that *apple* goes with *a*, *ball* with *b* and *cat* with *c*.
6   Recognises and says the number *1* and understands the amount.
7   Can hold a pencil correctly and colour a picture.

Assessment key: A = excellent / above average. B = very good / age appropriate. C = can do task but not yet consistent. D = working towards this level.

Unit 2

Name	1	2	3	4	5	6	7	8

1 Can say the words for family members: *Mum, Dad, Grandma, Grandpa, me.*

2 Can perform the routine of tidying up the classroom.

3 Can say the sounds, sing the names and trace the letters *d*, *e* and *f*.

4 Recognises that *doll* goes with *d*, *elephant* with *e* and *fish* with *f*.

5 Recognises and says the number *2* and understands the amount.

6 Can understand that some buildings are made from brick.

7 Recognises and says the colour *red* and is aware of the shape *square*.

8 Contributed to a *Learning Stars* corner in the classroom.

Assessment key: A = excellent / above average. B = very good / age appropriate. C = can do task but not yet consistent. D = working towards this level.

Little Learning Stars Teacher's Guide

Unit 3

Name	1	2	3	4	5	6	7	8

1 Can say the classroom words: *crayon, book, pencil, table, chair.*
2 Can perform the classroom routine of pushing their chair under the table quietly.
3 Can say the sounds, sing the names and trace the letters *g*, *h* and *i.*
4 Recognises that *goat* goes with *g*, *hat* with *h* and *insect* with *i.*

5 Recognises and says the number *3* and understands the amount.
6 Recognises which everyday items are made from wood.
7 Recognises and says the colour *yellow* and is aware of the shape *triangle*.
8 Can make a finger print picture of Bella.

Assessment key: A = excellent / above average. B = very good / age appropriate. C = can do task but not yet consistent. D = working towards this level.

Little Learning Stars Teacher's Guide

Unit 4

Name	1	2	3	4	5	6	7

1 Can say the words for toys: *kite, ball, teddy, train, doll*.
2 Can perform the classroom routine of putting rubbish in the bin and recognises which items are rubbish and which are not.
3 Can say the sounds, sing the names and trace the letters *j, k* and *l*.
4 Recognises that *jelly* goes with *j, kite* with *k* and *lemon* with *l*.
5 Recognises and says the number *4* and understands the amount.
6 Can understand which things move and which do not.
7 Recognises and says the colour *green* and is aware of the shape *circle*.

Assessment key: A = excellent / above average. B = very good / age appropriate. C = can do task but not yet consistent. D = working towards this level.

105

Unit 5

Name	1	2	3	4	5	6	7

1 Can say the animal words: *cat, hen, rabbit, bird*.
2 Can perform the classroom routine of putting away their books and can differentiate between big and small books and where they go.
3 Can say the sounds, sing the names and trace the letters *m, n, o* and *p*.
4 Recognises that *mouse* goes with *m*, *nest* with *n*, *orange* with *o* and *pizza* with *p*.
5 Recognises and says the numbers *5* and *6* and understands the amounts.
6 Recognises that some animals are awake at night: *owl, bat* and *fox*.
7 Recognises and says the colour *blue* and is aware of the shape *rectangle*.

Assessment key: A = excellent / above average. B = very good / age appropriate. C = can do task but not yet consistent. D = working towards this level.

Unit 6

Name	1	2	3	4	5	6	7

1 Can say the food and drink words: *juice, sandwich, grapes, apple, water, cake*.
2 Can perform the routine of washing and drying their hands.
3 Can say the sounds, sing the names and trace the letters *q, r, s, t*.
4 Recognises that *queen* goes with *q*, *rabbit* with *r*, *sun* with *s* and *tomato* with *t*.

5 Recognises and says the numbers *7* and *8* and understands the amounts.
6 Can understand how bread is made and recognises different forms of bread.
7 Recognises and says the colour *white* and is aware of a cloud shape.

Assessment key: A = excellent / above average. B = very good / age appropriate. C = can do task but not yet consistent. D = working towards this level.

Unit 7

Name	1	2	3	4	5	6	7

1 Can say the clothes words: *shoes, socks, trousers, skirt, T-shirt*.
2 Can perform the routine of taking their shoes off inside and putting them on to go out.
3 Can say the sounds, sing the names and trace the letters *u, v* and *w*.
4 Recognises that *umbrella* goes with *u, van* with *v* and *window* with *w*.
5 Recognises and says the number *9* and understands the amount.
6 Recognises the difference between the emotions and can say the words *happy* and *sad*.
7 Recognises and says the colour *black* and is aware of the shape *diamond*.

Assessment key: A = excellent / above average. B = very good / age appropriate. C = can do task but not yet consistent. D = working towards this level.

Unit 8

Name	1	2	3	4	5	6	7	8

1   Can say the words for rooms: *bedroom, bathroom, kitchen, living room.*
2   Can say where they are: *I'm in the (bedroom).*
3   Shows an appreciation of their own home.
4   Can say the sounds, sing the names and trace the letters *x, y* and *z.*

5   Recognises that *fox* goes with *x, yo-yo* with *y* and *zebra* with *z.*
6   Can sing the complete *Alphabet* song with support.
7   Recognises and says the number *10* and understands the amount.
8   Can distinguish between hot and cold.

Assessment key: A = excellent / above average. B = very good / age appropriate. C = can do task but not yet consistent. D = working towards this level.

Little Learning Stars Teacher's Guide

Notes

Notes

Notes